MW01195461

A PRIMER FOR GAMEMASTERS

ARBITER OF WORLDS

FOREWORD BY COURTNEY CAMPBELL

ALEXANDER MACRIS

ARBITER OF WORLDS
A PRIMER FOR GAMEMASTERS
By Alexander Macris
Foreword by Courtney Campbell

Arbiter of Worlds ©2018 Autarch™ LLC. Adventurer Conqueror King System © 2011-2018 Autarch LLC. The Auran Empire™ and all proper names, dialogue, plots, storylines, locations, and characters relating thereto are copyright 2011-2018 by Alexander Macris and used by Autarch LLC under license. This material is protected under the copyright laws of the United States of America. Any reproduction or unauthorized use of the material or artwork contained herein is prohibited without the written permission of the copyright owners. Autarch™, Adventurer Conqueror King™, Adventurer Conqueror King System™, Arbiter of Worlds™ and ACKS™ are trademarks of Autarch™ LLC.

This book is dedicated to Gary Gygax, David Arneson, Tom Moldvay, Zeb Cook, Greg Stafford, Steve Perrin, Ken St. Andre, Marc Miller, Bob Bledsaw, Steve Jackson, and all the other great game designers who created our hobby. Thank you for making our lives better with your creativity and imagination.

CONTENTS

FOREWORD

There's nothing more useless than a book on how to run a game.

Usually they are put together by fans, who have little to no professional background, insufficient experience with technical writing, and are filled with bad advice and anecdotal stories to prove a tenebrous point.

It's arrogant to think that there's nothing to learn from books about running a game, but that view is reinforced the first couple times you check out such books, filled with egotistic examples of 'correct play'. When you're finished with such a treatise, and you put it down and realize you didn't learn one new thing and simply have your blood pressure up, because the balls of this guy—publishing a guide on how to run a game!

There's always an exception though. This book is the exception.

I've been gaming for over 3 decades, running one or two games a week for nearly that whole stretch. I'm a professional in the literal field of adventure creation and presentation. What can this book teach me?

A lot, actually.

It's not only Alex's varied life experience and technical expertise that make this such a superb read. He makes his points the way you would expect a Harvard trained lawyer to do. It's the fact that if you read this book, you are going to come out knowing real things you did not know before that will help you run games at the table.

It's good for new gamemasters, because it tersely and incontrovertibly covers the basics that everyone should know, e.g. fudging is bad, but it's ok to save five minutes at the end of a combat by doing so. But it also contains definitive and irrefutable answers about both the original source of alignment as well as how to concretely use it as a tool in play, the specific methods via which random generation inspires emergent play, and methods of designing and structuring play around the agency of the participants.

It's worth the cover price alone to be able to show it to a player who wants to argue that 'his character would do that' based on his alignment.

I finished it like a pleasant surprise. I had a tool I can use during play, I learned things I didn't know before, and my blood pressure wasn't elevated at all. What a wonderful world!

In reflection, it's not terribly surprising that the publisher of one of the most popular, well-written, and well-constructed versions of classic *Dungeons & Dragons* would write an equally useful guide to running games.

Because I've been gaming for so long, I'm always looking for the long-tail products. Those innovations that stay useful no matter whether you're playing a game from 1979 or one from 2019. *Cities* by Midkemia Press. *Book of War* by Daniel Collins. *The Wilderness Alphabet* by Jim Pacek. *On the Non-Player Character* by me. *Aurora's Whole Realms Catalogue* by Anne Brown and J. Robert King.

And now, Arbiter of Worlds by Alexander Macris.

I'm a little bit jealous you get to read it for the first time. Enjoy!

-Courtney Campbell

CHAPTER 1

MASTER OF THE GAME

"Quis custodiet ipsos custodies?" - Juvenal, Roman poet, 2nd c. AD

Whether you've played a tabletop role-playing game or not, you probably are familiar with the concept of the Dungeonmaster (DM) or Gamemaster (GM). They're sometimes also called Judges, Referees, or Storytellers. Whatever they're called, they are the hardy souls who organize the play group, run the campaign, and judge the sessions. Indeed, Wizards of the Coast considers DMs their "lifeblood," explaining, "You learn D&D because somebody teaches you how to play. And that somebody is usually a Dungeonmaster."

The great Juvenal asked: "Who watches the watchmen?" I ask: Who teaches the GM how to GM? Generally, the answer is "nobody." And that's a problem. I've long believed that one of the major obstacles impeding the spread of the tabletop hobby is the lack of good GMs. It's been my experience that most people who like games, given the chance, will participate in a tabletop RPG, and once they start participating, continue to enjoy it. But most people don't get to ever even try an RPG, simply because there is a worldwide shortage of Gamemasters.

As a tabletop patriot, I ask not what RPGs can do for me, but what I can do for RPGs. This book is my answer. It's my guidance on how to run your own game. I'm going to teach the teachers - so that you can go forth and start your own campaigns, and spread the tabletop RPG pastime. I will teach you to be a judge, a storyteller, an adversary, and a worldbuilder **– an arbiter of worlds.**

In this book, I'm going to focus my attention primarily on the fantasy genre. Why? Partly it's because fantasy is the most popular genre. Fantasy games like *Dungeons & Dragons*® and *Pathfinder*® are almost everybody's introduction to the hobby. Partly, it's because fantasy is my favorite genre, and the one I've worked in most often professionally as the designer and publisher of the *Adventurer Conqueror King System*. That's not to say that a lot of the discussion in this book won't apply to other genres of tabletop RPG, such as science fiction, post-apocalyptic, superheroes, or horror. It will! Here and there throughout the book I even offer some suggestions about how to use some of these ideas in other genres. It's just not the primary lens we'll be viewing the subject through.

THE FOUNDATION OF GAMEMASTERING

Let's start with the foundation of gamemastering. It's not what you think.

As I mention above, a GM has many responsibilities, ranging from teaching new players, to organizing the group, to judging the sessions. The manifold role of the GM is precisely what makes it so intimidating for new entrants - there are few people who feel comfortable organizing what is in essence a social club, and doing improvisational acting, and being a rules lawyer, and being a story writer, and so on. The many roles of the GM have also contributed to the manifold names for the same job.

One common name for a GM is "Storyteller," a legacy of White Wolf's *Storyteller* RPG system. Unfortunately, I believe White Wolf did the profession of GM an incalculable harm when it said that a person running one of their popular games was called a "Storyteller." It's a name that suggests that your primary role will be telling a story, and this mantra created an entire generation of gamers who sneered at preparation, judging, and game mechanics, and who viewed their chief job as improvisational literature. The result: at best, melodramatic amateur theatre. At worst, entire groups turned off by a not-game with no rules.

Storytelling is indeed a function of the gamemaster, and it's the one most people think they are signing up to fill. But it's actually just one of several functions, and it is in many ways the least important. It is certainly the farthest from the foundation of the GM role.

So if not storytelling, what lies at the essence of being a GM? Role playing games descended from miniature wargaming. Miniature wargames are competitive simulations, generally with two opposed teams - say, Germany and Russia in World War II. But most miniature wargames also have a participant called a "judge" or "referee." The role of the judge in a miniature wargame is:

- To choose or create the scenario the other players will compete within

- To help explain, teach, and enforce the rules

- To prevent cheating and keep the players honest

- To rule on "grey areas" not covered by the rules

- To control the flow of information to permit "fog of war"

Note what's absent from the role of a miniature wargame judge: While today the GM is often perceived as "the adversary," a miniature wargame judge was not responsible for playing the adversary - he was, in fact, a neutral referee between the adversaries (i.e., the players).

And so it was in the first role playing games; the GM was not responsible for playing the adversaries, either. In Dave Arneson's Blackmoor campaign, for instance, the players were initially pitted against each other - one of them was a vampire named Sir Fang, while another was a cleric - with Arneson serving as the arbiter.

Nor was the miniature wargame judge responsible for telling a story. A story might emerge over the course of a miniature wargame, but it does so by happenstance, as a result of the unfolding of the battle. When the game is over, a story - or, really, a fictional "military history" - could be written up. But the judge did not write it up in advance, or adjust the course of the game to have one side win or lose based on the plot.

Likewise, in early tabletop RPGs, the judges did not have a "story" for their game. They had a setting and a set of rules, and the outcome was left up to the players. The original RPG, *Braunstein* (which preceded D&D by several years), was explicitly an open-ended wargame, and ended up going in directions its creator never foresaw. (For more on the origins of D&D, see the authoritative book *Playing at the World* by Jon Peterson.)

The foundation and first function of the GM was then, and is now, Judge. You show me a player who knows the rules, can teach them to others, is comfortable making rulings in grey areas, and can control information flow between players as necessary, and I'll show you a player who is on his way to being a great GM.

There are three other functions. The second function is Worldbuilder, a function that arose out of wargame judging ("choose or create the scenario"), and expanded over time as games became richer and more detailed. The other two, as I've already mentioned, are ancillary to the core. These are Adversary and Storyteller."

Next chapter, we'll start to explore these functions in more detail, but for now your homework is to pick up your favorite rules - maybe a starter set if you don't have any rules yet - and start mastering them.

CHAPTER 2

JUDGING THE GAME

In writing this book, I set out to teach the art of building and running fantasy RPG campaigns to aspiring GMs (gamemasters). My premise in doing so is that the growth of the tabletop RPG hobby depends on gamemasters to organize the play group, run the campaign, and judge the sessions. Because this is a challenging job, there is a perpetual shortage of GMs, and as such there are many people who would play RPGs if there were a GM to run them. With this premise in mind, I then discussed the origin of the Gamemaster role, and laid out the 4 functions of the Gamemaster:

1. Judge

2. Worldbuilder

3. Adversary

4. Storyteller

I called storytelling "in many ways the least important" function, and assigned the Judging function as the first, basic role. But before I plunge into an explanation of the importance of Judging, I want to respond to some common criticisms I have historically received on my position.

It's Not Your Job to Make Sure People Have Fun

When I list the four functions of the GM, the most common response I get is that I'm totally wrong – because "the real job of the GM is to make sure people have fun."

Well, I disagree!

If you're the GM, it's **not** your job to **make sure** people have fun. The belief that when a player doesn't have fun it's means the GM has failed has caused more GMs more grief and heartburn than any other myth in gaming. You can be an amazing GM, yet a player might not have fun. Because whether or not people have fun is going to depend on factors that are outside your control: How did their spouse treat them on their way over? How was their day at work? How well do they roll the dice? Do they play the game as well as the other players? You can't control these things, and therefore you shouldn't feel responsible for them. This is Stoicism 101.

What you should feel responsible for doing is creating an **environment** in which everyone **could** have fun. Imagine that you are hosting a party: Your job is to provide the right mix of appetizers, drinks, ambiance, and crowd so that people can have fun. It's not to act like a clown because Rob had a bad day at work. This is a subtle point, but if you keep it in mind, you'll avoid a lot of self-inflicted doubt and stress about your role.

The Agency Theory of Fun

So how do you create an environment in which everyone could have fun? I hope you won't mind a theoretical answer to this question. It involves a concept that I'll call "the agency theory of fun."

In philosophy, agency is the capacity for human beings to make choices and to impose those choices on the world. It's my belief that in our everyday lives, humans in modern society feel an absence of agency. Most of our capacity for meaningful choice is illusory; our daily lives are routine, and our scope of choice limited by lack of opportunity or resources. Very few people really can "change the world" in even a small way. Almost all of us lock on to meaningless decisions, such as what football team to support, or what color to dye our hair, as a means of expressing our need for agency. (Incidentally, cognitive scientists who have studied such matters have found that intelligent people can feel the lack of agency more poignantly than most, and often experience a sense of existential depression as a result. For more on this, see the fascinating book *Misdiagnosis and Dual Diagnoses of Gifted Children and Adults* by James Webb and Edward Amend).

In any case, I believe the great enjoyment elicited by tabletop RPGs (and some videogames) is a result of creating a sense of agency among their players. In an RPG, by making choice X, the player can impose result Y, which is the essence of agency. And because tabletop RPGs are an experience shared within a meaningful social circle of friends and colleagues, result Y feels meaningful. In the context of your circle of friends, Nick *really did* save Erik's life last week. Moreover, because tabletop RPGs are enjoyed sequentially, in a campaign format, the number of choices made and the impact of those choices compounds over time. The game becomes more meaningful the longer it is experienced. This is why long-term campaigns are more fun than one-off sessions, and why playing with a bunch of close friends is more fun than playing solitaire or with a group of strangers. Sustained campaigns with close friends create a stronger sense of agency.

However, in order for a campaign to effectively create a sense of agency, the players must be able to make real (not faux) choices that have meaningful consequences on the players and their world. And that's a requirement which is in direct opposition to storytelling, or making sure everyone has fun.

A Roller Coaster May Be a Wild Ride, but It Is Still a Railroad

Imagine that your party has only a few minutes to find the artifact that can close the gate to the abyss. The artifact could be underneath the dark citadel, or on the peak of the lonely mountain - but they don't have time to search both. Now, if you have real choice, the artifact is really in one location or the other, and your choice will determine whether or not you find it. On the other hand, if you have faux choice, then you only think you have choice. Whichever choice you make, that will be where the artifact is, along with an interesting, pre-scripted encounter of your level forcing you to fight to get it. So in the latter instance either choice is fun - but both are faux.

Many GMs never offer real choice, because the problem with real choice is that players can only be sure they have real choice when they suffer meaningfully bad consequences. And in the context of a tabletop RPG, that usually means permanent destruction of something unique - a favored henchmen, irreplaceable magic artifact, animal companion, or player character.

For a while, a skilled sleight-of-hand artist can maintain suspension of disbelief about the reality of choice, leading players on a roller coaster ride that makes them think they are making real choices and facing meaningful consequences. It's the same art that a skilled novelist can use to make us believe that a favorite character is in danger, even though he's not. But a never-ending string of perfect, dramatically appropriate, fun outcomes that defies probability eventually leads even the dimmest players to realize they don't have real choice at all. A roller coaster may be a wild ride, but it's still a railroad. And when the railroading gets revealed, the sense of agency dies, and with it dies the sense of fun.

So this, then, is the paradox of gamemastering: In order to make sure that everybody could have fun, you have to be willing to let the players make choices that lead to results that aren't fun. You can't guarantee the fun. And if you try to make sure everyone has fun, eventually you'll guarantee that no one has fun at all, because you'll destroy the sense of agency which is the root of the hobby's pleasure.

AGENCY AND CAUSALITY, OR WHY RULES MATTER

The agency theory of fun also explains why rules matter. Rules, in a tabletop RPG, are ultimately about what philosophers call action, where "action" means intentional effects caused by an agent. It is the rules that dictate the results of action, and thus define the relationship between a player's choices and the consequence he experiences. The rules provide the framework of cause and effect that gives meaning to choice. For instance, virtually every RPG has rules that dictate when you may choose to attack a target, how the success or failure of this attack are determined, and the consequences of each.

A game without rules cannot provide a sense of agency, anymore than a world without causality can. If the players operate subject to arbitrary outcomes - what the ancients called "Acts of God" and RPG designers call "GM Fiat" - they have no meaningful way of knowing or understanding what the consequences of their choices will be, and thus no agency.

I believe that the agency theory of fun explains why esoteric games like Amber Diceless Roleplaying or Everway have never caught on, and why as games evolve, they tend to evolve in the direction of more rules.

Comprehensible, detailed rules add to the player's sense of agency, just as playing with friends in an ongoing campaign does. (This does not mean that extremely complex games like Rolemaster are an unmitigated good - but that's a critique for another time. Let's just say that the simplest rule system that succeeds at providing agency is best.)

Agency also explains why dice are, and will always be, a popular mechanic with RPGs. As I explained above with the example of the hidden artifact, if the consequences are pre-determined, then the choice is not real. The inherent contradiction between omniscience and free will has plagued religion for thousands of years, and it plagues RPGs, too. For instance, imagine if tabletop RPG combat went like this:

> Player: "I attack the dragon."
>
> GM: "Based on your attack bonus and the dragon's armor class, if you attack, you are certain to miss."
>
> Player: "Uh... well I don't attack, then."

It's hard to imagine that game being much fun because the results of the player's choices are determined before he's made them. (This is the same reason that Tic-Tac-Toe isn't fun.) Agency, then, requires that we be able to predict the consequences of our choices, but not with certainty. D&D creates agency with its Core Mechanic: "To determine if your character success at a task, you roll a d20, add any relevant modifiers and compare the result to a target number. If the result equals or exceeds the target number, your character succeeds. If the result is lower, you fail." The relevant modifiers and the target number provide causality. The d20 provides uncertainty. Both are essential.

DON'T CHANGE THE DICE, CHANGE THE RULES

Because randomness is inherent to RPGs, every gamemaster soon becomes familiar with the temptation to cheat, or in gamer parlance, "fudge the dice." For instance, imagine that a new player, Carrie, is joining your campaign. In her very first battle, her character takes a critical hit, and is killed. The temptation will be very strong to pretend that the die roll was different - that a critical hit was just a normal hit, or even a miss. Especially if you think "my job is to make sure Carrie has fun," you'll convince yourself that dying is not fun, and that therefore Carrie's character shouldn't die.

The agency theory says that you should never fudge a meaningful die roll. The desire to fudge is founded on the faulty premise that you need to make sure people have fun. But it's a mistake to believe that letting a character die destroys fun. In fact, the opposite is true - it's fudging the dice that destroys fun, by destroying the ability for the players to make meaningful choices. Letting the player live when her choices would have led to her death is ultimately destructive to the game's fun, for all the reasons I explained earlier.

So what do you do about Carrie above? It depends. If Carrie died because she rushed in to a fight that she shouldn't have, or volunteered to take point, then you let her die. But if she died because she got killed by an invisible sniper before she even knew what was happening, the answer is "change the rules in advance to prevent that sort of situation from happening."

For instance, in the original edition of D&D, characters died instantly when they reach 0 hit points, and since starting characters could begin with as little as 1 hit point, that meant that death could come at almost any time, almost arbitrarily. There are several ways to resolve this dilemma. The classic approach was to maintain what one popular RPG blogger calls "ironic distance" during the early levels - the knowledge that you're not really your character. Early D&D supported this with quick and dirty character generation that let you replace your dead fighter with another fighter in about 30 seconds.

As D&D developed, though, the desire for increased player agency lead to ever-increasing levels of character customization, making choices that impacted what the character was like. This investment made it harder for players to maintain sufficient distance from their characters to tolerate arbitrary death. D&D's designers quickly introduced mechanics to address this, most famously by allowing characters to be "dying but not dead" until they actually hit -10 hit points. With a "dying but not yet dead" mechanic, then Carrie's party still has a chance to save her by defeating the sniper and healing her wounds.

In real life, many things can happen to us that really are the result of "Acts of God," and have nothing to do with our agency. There is, after all, a slim probability that sitting at my desk typing this article, I will be killed by a falling meteorite. And that sucks! In fact, the very abundance of these types of events is exactly what strips us of our sense of agency in day-to-day life. Since RPG rules are fun to the extent that they give the player a sense of agency, mechanics that strip away agency should be changed. The evolution of the classic D&D game shows us how this works. When you encounter rules in your favorite RPG that strip away player agency, you should change them, too.

CHAPTER 3
IT'S NOT YOUR STORY

In the last chapter, I explained the agency theory of fun, and showed how by focusing on objective rules, honest dice, and player choice, you maximize the fun for your players in the long term. In this chapter, I want to turn our attention to that most contentious of subjects - story.

Now, in arguing that judging, not storytelling, is the most important facet of gamemastering, I have not been arguing against a straw man. I've been arguing against the mainstream school of gamemastering of the past decades, which teaches that story is the most important function of the GM. This viewpoint reached perhaps its fullest elucidation in the *3.5 Dungeon Masters Guide II*. Let's take a look at that formulation now, because it illustrates everything that's wrong with the mainstream view.

THE WORST ADVICE EVER GIVEN

The *DMG II* divides campaigns into two possible structures, "episodic" and "continuity." While admitting to the possibility of episodic campaigns, it notes that since they are just "composed of unrelated adventures" they are best reserved for groups with "spotty attendance," "oddball behavior," and "reactive players who like to have their objectives supplied to them." The real action happens in continuity campaigns, where "one adventure leads to another, creating an overall **story arc** that builds over time... You will adapt adventures created by others into **your story arc**." [Emphasis added].

The *DMG II* never mentions episodic campaigns again. Instead, it moves on to an entire section devoted to how to end your campaign, noting that a campaign with a fixed ending "increases the sense of excitement," adding that "any entertainer knows to **leave the audience** wanting more." [Emphasis added.] The authors offer several pages of advice on how to close your campaign, of which this was the most telling:

> Plan carefully to see that the conclusive scenes of a closed campaign pay off. By centering the entire campaign on a set of victory conditions, you're promising a big, exciting finish. Prepare that final sequence exhaustively. It must be exquisitely balanced... Set up the climactic sequence so your resident tacticians have no chance to reconnoiter or plan in advance. Design the encounter with options that allow you to adjust its difficulty on the fly... When in doubt, fudge die rolls shamelessly, feigning surprise at the results.

The inherent assumption here, of course, is that the GM is a wise, smart entertainer, and the players are his audience and along for the ride - nuisances who will attempt to ruin your ending with their "reconnaissance" and "planning." The prior chapter has already explained in detail why you should disregard everything written above, but I think it's worth translating the language above for you into how I read it:

> Plan carefully to see that the conclusive scenes of a closed campaign arbitrarily end the way you want them to. By centering the entire campaign on a set of victory conditions, you're putting yourself in a situation where you have to railroad the ending, so you'd better prepare that final sequence exhaustively. It must be exquisitely balanced so that they almost lose, but then win, no matter what choices they make. Set up the climactic sequence so your resident

tacticians have no path except your path, no matter how much they want to choose otherwise. Ignore any sense of fairness to the players, and design the encounter with options that allow you to arbitrarily make it harder or easier for the players so that they end up doing what you want, how you want. When in doubt, lie to your players about what you rolled and just make up an outcome you think is better.

Of course, the moment your players realize you are doing any of the above, the whole effort becomes a sham - they can't be excited about it because they know that they're really just an audience, not a participant. That's the complete opposite of the lesson of agency from the previous chapter: The players should be participants, not spectators.

The good news is that GMing doesn't have to be this way. You don't have to get trapped into a false dichotomy of "episodic" versus "continuous," nor do you need to force players to drive down your Epic Story Superhighway in order to run a fun campaign. **There is a better way.**

WHAT HAPPENS NEXT - OR WHAT JUST HAPPENED?

But first, let's define some concepts. The *DMG II* is quick to advise gamemasters to have a "story arc," but it never stops to define what a story arc is. We will: A story arc is a meta-story that links individual storylines together. Stories, of course, are as old as mankind, but not every story is part of a story arc. Consider the early Greek myths of Perseus slaying the Medusa, and of Bellerophon slaying the Chimera. Each has a story "line," but there is no link between the two. In contrast, consider the later myths of Paris wooing Helen of Troy, Achilles slaying Hector, and Odysseus encountering Circe - these are all linked by the "Trojan War" story arc. For a more recent example, contrast the adventures of Robert Howard's

Conan (short stories without a story arc) with Tolkien's Bilbo and Frodo (adventures within a larger story arc).

Many people's earliest experiences of role-playing games are similar to those early Greek myths or Conan short stories. The party of adventurers goes to the dungeon, knocks down some doors, kills some orcs, and goes home. Next week's adventure, they knock down some thicker doors, kill some ogres, and so on. The first published RPG products that actually linked adventures across space and time was Gary Gygax's G-D-Q series of modules (*Against the Giants* leading to *Vault of the Drow* culminating in *Queen of the Demonweb Pits*). But the big breakthrough came when TSR gave us the *Dragonlance* series, which featured a story arc over a dozen modules long. Popular D&D blogger James Maliszewski has described *Dragonlance* as gaming's *Lord of the Rings*, and with good reason.

To players in the mid 80s, story arcs were revolutionary, adding highly detailed backstory, depth, and a sense of purpose to what had previously been only loosely connected modules. And those are all wonderful things, things that any good gamemaster should strive to have in his games. But there was a hidden cost to the story arc: a cost in player agency. A story arc only works if the narrator can create a plot - that is: a sequence of events that effects change on the situation of his protagonists. If the narrator is a gamemaster, then the players are his protagonists, and he's made a commitment to effecting change on them. The players are now the objects, rather than subjects, of a story. A story arc transforms adventurers and agents into actors and audience.

For this reason, I call campaigns that use a story arc "directed stories." The gamemaster, like a stage or movie director, is directing the sequence of events that will occur with an eye towards achieving particular outcomes or expressing particular themes. It is story focused on what happens next. The opposite of directed story is "emergent story," story focused on what just happened. Emergent story is the memoirs of your fictional characters, and the history of their fictional deeds.

A directed story GM is concerned with whether or not what the players are doing is moving things in the direction the gamemaster desires. An emergent story GM is concerned with whether or not the players are succeeding in moving things in the direction **they** desire.

A directed story GM is a fortune teller who predicts that awesome things will happen to you in the future. An emergent story GM is a bard who weaves a story about the awesome things that you made happen.

A WEB, NOT AN ARC

Emergent story does not happen in a vacuum. You cannot simply release your players into the Forgotten Realms and expect entertainment to ensue - or if entertainment does ensue, it will likely be very short term and involve inns, bar brawls, or orcs. Emergent story needs its own version of the story arc, but one catered to emergent play. The technique I use to allow emergent storytelling is something I call a "story web."

My approach is geographical - location based, rather than event based. I begin by sketching out a map of the playspace within which the campaign will launch (a "sandbox"), and developing about ten to twenty points of interest within it. If you're running D&D, the sandbox could be a wilderness map with 6-mile hexes, similar to the recent *Points of Light* accessory. If you were playing *Classic Traveller*, it could be a sub-sector map of star systems. For *Call of Cthulhu*, it might be a map of London circa 1929. Each point of interest in the sandbox initially gets a paragraph of description.

The actual process of creating the points of interest is a mix of free-form creativity, adaptation/borrowing of other published material, rolls on random encounter charts, or other techniques. Here's an example from my own Auran Empire campaign of a point of interest, #18: Shrine of the White Lady:

> Hidden in a secluded forest clearing is an ivy-covered shrine of white marble, sacred to Mityara, built by the dawn elves before the Argollëan War. The shrine is guarded by a unicorn. Within the shrine is a pool of crystal clear water. Characters who drink from the waters enjoy the benefits of a *cure serious wounds* spell.

Once I've sketched out my points of interest, I go back and I look for possible links between them - proximity, shared history, etc. The idea is that since story is going to emerge from the characters encountering interesting stuff, the story web should help them move from one point of interest to another.

In my Auran Empire campaign, my initial points of interest included four different ruins that were all historically linked to the fallen elven kingdom. I decided to link them in game by placing a special pool in each location that showed where the other ruins could be found:

> The surface of the pool is a mosaic map of the old elven kingdoms, which shows the location of the elven ruins located at #7, #10, #13, and #18.

Other ways players could uncover links between locations in my sandbox included finding treasure maps in hoards that lead to another point of interest; rescuing captives that hail from another place; translating hieroglyphic carvings on the wall that mention another point of interest;

reading NPC journals about other locations; talking to NPCs who traveled between the two locations; and so on. (If any of you have ever designed a computer RPG or MMOG, of course, you'll note that the above process is not that far removed from how quest chains are created.)

Because D&D is very sensitive to the level of characters, I structured my initial story web such that the interlinked strands did not have any direct links from low to high level locations. Since the web is essentially a road map of interest for the players, you don't want to purposefully lead them to destruction. This "bundled" structure of linking is also beneficial in that you can launch the campaign with only 3-4 of the points of interest ready in detail, rather than having to get all of them done up front.

What contrasts the story web from the story arc is that it offers two different layers of choice. The first layer of choice is that at any point the party has multiple threads of the web to pursue. Do they want to see where the treasure map leads, or visit the elven ruins they learned about from the mosaic? The second layer of choice is the ability for the party to ignore the web entirely. Since the points of interest exist independently as locations in my game world, the party can go explore as it would like. In short, the story web is a road network to a range of destinations, not a railroad track leading down one way.

Of course, if the party can go anywhere - and you only have the first 3-4 points of interest ready to go - that does provide certain challenges. My solution to the challenges has been twofold. First, I tend to sketch out (or use pre-existing) one page descriptions of the points of interest I haven't created in detail. Even if they end up somewhere I never expected, I have something to go on.

Second, I create a wandering encounter chart that features many powerful and interesting encounters on it. A solid wandering encounter chart can make the travel from Point A to Point B itself be a fulfilling session of gaming. More importantly, if the wandering encounter chart is scaled for the average level of play, rather than the starting level of play, it will implicitly persuade you party to stick to more civilized areas early on. For instance, most of the encounters on my chart are at 5th-7th level of difficulty. Beneath 5th level, exploration of unknown areas is risky venture, not to be done lightly; far safer to follow the map. But at 8th level and above, the random encounters begin to seem less threatening, and the campaign setting "opens up" organically to more freeform activity. But all of this is done without ever forcing any choice or outcome on the player. They can, if they wish, break out into new or unexpected directions (and my players sure have, sometimes)!

DON'T BE A PLOT NAZI

With a story web, you can't be sure that your players will encounter #1 before #2, or #2 before #10. Nor can you be sure they'll encounter any particular location, character, or monster at all. You have established a setting, but the story that occurs within that setting will be the result of player choice. They will be enjoying an emergent story as they move along the strands of your story web. Or burn your story web to the ground, as the case may be.

At a certain point in the course of running your campaign, I guarantee that you'll begin to feel the urge to transform the emergent story into a directed story. You'll say to yourself, "The Lost Temple of Arneson is so cool! I really want them to go there." And so the local King will come down with Bubonic Ebola, which will only be cured if the Polyhedral of Power can be recovered from the Lost Temple. Now, there's nothing wrong with this per se; I use a set of random charts to create background events in my setting, for instance, and one of them really can inflict pestilence on the population.

But to stay true to player agency, you need to be willing to let your players say, "Nah. I'd rather go check out the Tower of Gygax. Pass the King our best wishes for his recovery," and run with what they want to do. Maybe that means the King dies and the land is in upheaval. Maybe it means that another adventurer recovers the Polyhedral, and the PCs suddenly have rivals for their fame in the land. Maybe it means that the King declares them outlaws and they join forces with the monsters. Again, the point is that the story isn't something the GM decides alone. The story emerges from what the players decide. GMs who force their players to pursue one particular plot are being dictators when they should be democrats. Don't be a Plot Nazi and force your story arc on them. After all, the first Indiana Jones movie showed you what happens to Nazis when they mess with Arcs.

CHAPTER 4
THE GAMEMASTER IS SATAN

Chapter 3 discussed how a gamemaster should weave a story based on what has happened in the campaign, rather than what he wants to happen, and offered a technique for building story webs for emergent narrative. In this chapter, we'll be setting aside talk of story to discuss the gamemaster's role as the adversary.

THE GM IS GOD - BUT HE PLAYS SATAN

The GM is God – or, at least, he is god of the world he has created. With pen and mouse, he can raise and lower mountain ranges, bring ruin to great civilizations, change the climate, unleash catastrophes. Within the context of the game, the gamemaster has powers worthy of the Old Testament. But that god-like omnipotence must sometimes be set aside, so that the gamemaster can adopt another Biblical role.

In Hebrew, the word for adversary is "satan," and throughout the Hebrew tradition, the various military and legal adversaries of the characters are always called the Satan. The role of the Satan in this tradition is always to test the protagonists to his fullest extent, even though God, who created Satan in the first place and assigned him to this task, is secretly hoping the protagonists will succeed in overcoming these tests. Most famously, the Satan appears in the Book of Job as an agent of God, whose role is to test the faith of the hapless hero. The Satan afflicts Job with loss of family, property, and health in order to tempt him to evil, but Job only gains character in the face of this adversity.

The Book of Job is wonderfully illustrative of the relationship between the GM's job as a whole and his specific role as adversary. The gamemaster, as god of the world he has created, creates various agents and uses them as adversaries to test his players with various challenges. Playing as the adversary, the gamemaster tests the protagonist to his fullest extent, and sometimes (playing as the adversary) defeats them, even though the gamemaster (being god of the game world) is always secretly hoping the protagonists will succeed in overcoming these tests.

DON'T MAKE THE ADVERSARY INTO A GOD

Now that I've given you a framework of Biblical proportions, the first thing you're going to need to do is create some adversaries to play. And here's where you are most likely to make your first big mistake: You'll make your adversary too godlike, too powerful. God didn't give Satan the power to just arbitrarily kill Job, but all too often, GMs give their main adversaries the power to arbitrarily kill the whole party. The rules of many games contribute to this.

Consider Sauron, the classic dark lord of fantasy fiction, and compare him to an 18th level Wizard in D&D 3.5. In order to learn the name of the thief (a 1st level halfling) who had his One Ring, Sauron was forced to torture it out of Gollum. He then had to have minions ride on horseback to the local village, to ask around for this fellow, and when they thought they had found him, they actually had to break into his inn and stab him with swords! In contrast, an 18th level Wizard in D&D could simply use *Discern Location* to find the ring, cast a quick *Greater Teleport* to its location, and then just *Power Word Kill* Frodo and take the damn thing. In other words, Sauron, who was a demigod, is way, way less powerful than a standard D&D wizard of not even epic level. That's pretty problematic if you want to create a villain in D&D or anything like it! Sauron is Satan, but an 18th-level D&D Wizard is God.

If you're running a game with a power level like D&D, and your arch-villains don't deal with your player characters in a similarly quick and convenient manner, you owe it to yourself and your players to explain why. There are only two basic explanations available to you:

- The adversaries are stupid.
- The adversaries don't have the power to dispatch the PCs.

In general, I think stupidity is a sub-optimal solution. It stretches the suspension of disbelief and reduces the sense of accomplishment by the players when they realize they only won because your villains were dumb-asses. It's why Obi-Wan Kenobi's victories over Darth Maul in *Episode I* and Anakin in *Episode III* are so unsatisfying: He only won because the Sith Lords were dumb-asses.

Unfortunately, stupidity is all too often the fallback for villains. Leaving aside the Darth brothers, let's take Ariakus, the arch-villain of Dragonlance. According to DL14 Dragons of Triumph, Ariakus is a 23rd-level Cleric / 10th level Fighter with 18 Wisdom - as wise as a man can possibly be! And yet, according to DL14, "Ariakus is so confident of his supreme abilities that he has a tendency to be careless when estimating the strength of his enemies. He does not give them credit for their skills, and consequently his plans may contain flaws that clever opponents may capitalize upon." That seems...unwise. And since Ariakus is both wise and powerful, we're left with an obviously stupid explanation as to why he doesn't just swat Tanis and Tasslehoff like the annoying gnats they are.

Some villains actually should be stupid, of course (all the ogres in the room, say "ho!"). But if your villain is supposed to be an evil genius, you should try to get rid of all of the following stupid justifications for his behavior: The villain is over-confident and does not see the heroes as a threat; the villain is too important to be bothered by the heroes, and dispatches minions instead; the villain is distracted by more pressing challenges; the villain is unaware of the heroes; the villain is toying with the heroes. If you haven't already, you really should read the Evil Overlord checklist.

So if we aren't going to rely on stupidity, how do we keep our villains adversarial rather than god-like?

The first is to change the rules. In my personal D&D 3.5 campaign, I substantially reduced the range and utility of all detection and teleportation magic for all characters for this very reason. Wizards are still deadly - they can blast lightning and hurl meteor swarms - but there are simply no magical spy satellites that can find people, and no way to beam across the continent. This has allowed me to have highly powerful villains that are still localized in their scope of threat. This approach works very well if you want to have lots of villains within a confined geography (it also makes hunt-and-fetch quests interesting again).

Another solution to the god-like villain is to leave him god-like, but begin your campaign with him somehow crippled at the outset. Over time his power increases, but so does that of the heroes. The early books of the *Wheel of Time* series did this beautifully, with a series of seals being broken, each break increasing the scope and power of the Dark One. This approach serves well for games with a leveling mechanic, since you can build a story web where the danger from the villain scales up as the heroes move through the web.

A third solution is to use a counter-force which checks the villain's power. I recently used this approach in a *Mutants & Masterminds* campaign. The arch-villain Mindbender could telepathically locate and kill anyone on the planet - a potential problem for the heroes, who could have all been killed in episode 1. My solution was to have an NPC mentor with precognitive powers that functioned with more precision from imminent and closely tied threats. This made it impossible for the arch-villain to directly attack the party without giving away his intent and location in advance - as a result, the villain was forced to use convoluted plans that never directly aimed at confronting the heroes. These plans were maddeningly fun to concoct, and fun for the players to unwind. (Note that if I hadn't limited the precognitive's powers to being tied to specific imminent threats against the party, I'd have created the god-like problem in reverse - i.e., how do you challenge a party that knows everything?)

THE PARABLE OF THE KING AND COURTESAN

I will close this chapter with a parable of a wise king who was concerned that his son lacked the moral character to rule. As a Biblical scholar, the king was familiar with the Book of Job, and he decided that he would test his son's character as God had tested Job's. So the king found the most beautiful courtesan in his harem and commanded her to attempt to seduce his son. To make the test challenging, he made sure the courtesan was beautiful, and told her that if she seduced his son, she would be queen. So motivated, she used all her charms on the hapless prince, yet when she failed to seduce the prince, the king was delighted.

The lesson for gamemasters should be clear: While you might play the courtesan, you are the king. You don't really want to screw your players; you just want to test their characters.

Next chapter we'll turn to the question of creating and playing adversaries with personality.

CHAPTER 5

ADVERSARIES ARE MADE OF PEOPLE!

Last chapter, I introduced the gamemaster as adversary, and cautioned against deploying the GM's god-like powers against the players. Now I'll turn to the question of who your adversaries should be, and how they should behave.

ADVERSARIES ARE MADE OF PEOPLE!

It seems an obvious point, but the best adversaries are people (loosely defined as "sapient creatures"). People generally find the challenges posed by other people to be the most interesting; witness the rise in the popularity of online gaming.

Of course, it's true that not every adversary needs to be a person. Dungeon traps are classic adversaries: They pose challenges that test the players' determination and cunning. Sometimes the environment itself is adversarial; natural disasters, wilderness obstacles, and catastrophic weather can all pose challenges to the players, but a campaign where the main villain is, for instance, an earthquake is likely to be an uninteresting campaign. Add an Elder Elemental Cult actively promoting the earthquake and fighting against the would-be heroes, and it gets more interesting again.

Still, even when the adversary is a person, it needn't be an enemy. An adversary just needs to be a character who poses challenges. The adversary could be a foil who serves to bring the protagonists into sharper focus. The adversary could be an ally who causes more trouble than their worth, like Lois Lane for Superman. Or it could be a rival from the same side who makes the heroes stay on top of their game. The latter is an under-utilized, but highly effective, adversary.

In my Auran Empire campaign, I created a rival adventuring party, "Imperial Vanguard," that wandered the map and cleared dungeons in regions near the PC adventurers. I introduced the Imperial Vanguard by having the players find their next dungeon already cleared of monsters, with a bold flag planted bearing the I.V. standard outside the entrance. Because the two parties weren't enemies per se - indeed, I.V. was technically an ally to the cause - the players could not simply confront and destroy them. That made I.V. even more challenging as adversaries. Without any possibility for direct confrontation, Imperial Vanguard suddenly became a factor in the party's every decision: Where should we explore to make sure we get there first? How long can we afford to rest without Imperial Vanguard cleaning the dungeon out before us? And so on. For a long time, the monsters in our campaign were just the means to the players' end of beating Imperial Vanguard.

ROLE-PLAY THE ADVERSARIES, DON'T WARGAME THEM

Creating interesting adversaries is only half the challenge, of course. The other half is playing them. Playing RPG adversaries is harder than it seems. Elsewhere in the book, I've criticized GMs who use their powers to railroad players into happy endings, fudging dice to make sure the players feel good, like bringing nerf chainsaws to the Thunderdome. But it's just as bad to go too far the other way. Especially when playing a miniatures-and-map RPG like D&D 4e, it's all too easy to treat encounters like wargames, with every adversary acting like a playing piece that's happy to sacrifice itself for the grand strategy. RPGs have wargame roots, so it's only natural for the GM to sometimes feel like he's playing a wargame. This is when it's wise to remember that the GM's wargame roots are as the neutral Judge, not as the Adversary. A GM who loses sight of this will inflict incalculable harm on a party he has totally outgunned.

For instance, he'll run opponents who'd rather fight to the last man than surrender, because the GM wants to inflict a few more hit points damage to weaken the party before the next encounter; leaders who can never be surprised by the party's tactics, because the GM allows his villains to know everything the GM knows; enemies who always attack as soon as the party splits up, because the GM wants to teach the players "never to split the party"; and so on.

A GM can always win if he wants to, and you don't prove anything by "beating" the players. But you do create an escalating level of antagonism between the GM and the players. For instance, I've seen players ask the GM to leave the room when they plan their strategy, for fear the GM will cheat and use what he knows against them. I've seen players refuse to tell the GM how many hit points their characters have left, so he can't have his minions target the weaker characters. Conditions like these are symptomatic of a campaign in which the game master has lost sight of his primary role (Judge) and gotten caught up in a secondary role (as Adversary).

The worst possible combination is an almost sadistic paternalism: The GM, relishing the pleasure of beating the players, uses the full scope of his powers to create and run impossible challenges, only to then fudge the dice to let the players win; usually letting them know he fudged it so that they can advance through "his" storyline the way the GM wants them to. This style of gamemastering was actually outlawed by the Geneva

Convention as a form of torture, but the US and UK weren't signatories to that chapter, and it continues to be practiced in some areas.

My preferred method of running adversaries is to role-play them. When I run orcs, they attack how the Dark Ages barbarians of the north were alleged to fight: in loose waves, berserk, initially heedless of casualties. If forced back enough by stout defense, their morale collapses, and they become easy prey to be mopped up. On the other hand, when I run were-rats, I attack only if I can ambush, retreat at the first sign of trouble, and surrender to save my furry hide if need be. And when I play a thousand-year old dragon, I plan carefully, move cautiously, and don't take any risks that could cost me my next thousand years.

And I never give the enemies knowledge they shouldn't have. For instance, the Cleric in our Auran Empire campaign secretly wore a Scarab of Protection that made him immune to death magic. Nevertheless, an evil lich that encountered the Cleric used death magic on the Cleric, because he posed the seemingly greatest threat to the lich. The lich didn't know that the Cleric was immune. (See my earlier notes on why your villains shouldn't have God-like omniscience!)

Doing it this way sometimes means that the NPCs don't behave in ways that would be considered tactically correct by a wargamer who knows everything the GM knows. Sometimes they'll surrender, even though if they'd have kept attacking, the monsters in the next room would have been able to defeat the party. Sometimes they'll run away, even though running away is just about the worst thing you can do in a battle (historically, 90% of all casualties were inflicted when the other side's morale broke).

This approach means the players can try kooky plans that would never fool the GM - but might fool the hill giants. It creates a more naturalistic, "real" world. And it can even turn fights into subtle clues to the nature of the opposition. "How did the were-rats know we were coming?" is a far more satisfying query if the answer is "because Steve the Retainer is a were-rat spy," rather than disassociated justification such as "this encounter will be more challenging if the player's ambush doesn't work." The beauty of playing the adversaries this way is that it also frees your players to participate in the experience as role-players, rather than wargamers.

CHAPTER 6
LET THERE BE LAW

In Chapter 5, I discussed who your adversaries should be, and how they should behave. Now let's turn our attention to the context within which both your player characters and your adversaries operate: the game world.

World building is my favorite part of gamemastering, but (despite the countless hours I devote to it), world building cannot be counted as the primary or even secondary role of the gamemaster. A GM can be an amazing judge, storyteller, and adversary without ever taking up the art of world-building. In fact, many gamemasters never create their own worlds or settings, instead relying on pre-established settings such as the *Forgotten Realms* or *Warhammer Universe*. Pre-established settings became popular within the first generation of the tabletop gaming hobby, and they have only increased in popularity since then. Nevertheless, I believe that even if you don't intend to create your own world, an understanding of the art of world building can only deepen your skills as a gamemaster; much the same way taking film classes can help you appreciate film even if you don't ever direct one. Whether you are crafting your own sandbox or running *D&D 5E* official materials, there's much to gain by studying the art of world building.

Start with Rules and Genre

There's a certain school of thought that says that the setting of a game, the genre of a game, and the rules of a game can all be divorced from each other. This school argues that one set of rules is just about as good as another, and all that counts are how the GM weaves it together. In fact, this premise underlies the rise of the D20 Open Gaming License in the 1990s. I'm not part of that school! I believe they have to form an organic whole.

As my third-year project at Harvard Law School (2000), I conducted a study on how the design of three different massively multiplayer games affected the societies of those games. To cut short a 100-page research paper, the answer was "strongly." It turns out that every set of game mechanics carries with it certain implicit and explicit assumptions about how the world works. They are the physical laws of the game world. Just like the law in the real world affects our societies, the laws in the fantasy world do, too.

While the research was for MMOGs, tabletop examples abound. For instance, *Cyberpunk 2020's* Interlock System offers a 10% chance for any given roll to be a critical success and a 10% chance for it to be a critical failure. *Cyberpunk 2020* therefore implies a world where any punk can get lucky, and even the best of the best are eventually going to bite it due to bad luck. If that's not how your world works, you don't want to use *Cyberpunk 2020* to run it. Because what will happen is that punks will get lucky, and even the best will die young.

Another example: *Classic Traveller* uses a fascinating character generation system in which players choose or are drafted into "careers" for their characters, such as army, marines, or merchants, and then spend anywhere from 4 to 20 years in service, graduating into play as seasoned experts. There's little to no character improvement thereafter. *Classic Traveller* therefore implies a world the opposite of the traditional "Heroic Myth" - age and experience trump youth. Young characters aren't potential heroes ready to unlock their potential; they are unskilled mooks. Luke Skywalker doesn't become a Jedi master, he dies. *Classic Traveller* also implies a world with lots of organized, institutional careers, diametrically opposed to the post-apocalyptic environment of most *D&D* campaigns. This is why so many efforts to use *Traveller* as *D&D* in space fail.

So before I begin building a world, I always decide what rules set I'll be using and what genre I'll be simulating. The choice of rules needs to be made simultaneously with the choice of genre. Some rules really can support multiple (if not all) settings and genres - Steve Jackson's *GURPS* and Chaosium's *Basic Roleplaying* come to mind. Other rules sets support particular genres marvelously, but fail spectacularly outside of them. Palladium Games' *RECON* might be a brilliant war movie RPG, but it's dreadful for heroic fantasy. *D&D* is great for heroic fantasy but lousy for investigative horror. Some rules sets are so narrowly tailored as to support not only just one genre, but just one setting; due to the career and magic system, it's hard to extract *Warhammer Fantasy* from the Old World setting, for instance.

It's possible to "hack" a rules set to support different genre conventions and settings, of course. And if you are trying to use a particular rules set (say, *D&D*) with a genre or setting it's not built for (say, the American Old West), you will need to. But with so many game systems available, and so many other challenges to gamemastering, it's probably better to find a game system that lines up with the genre and setting you want, at least initially, until you're ready to start tinkering with rules (a guilty pleasure of mine, discussed in depth in Chapter 18).

I personally find universal games like *GURPS* or *BRP* to be so broad as to make the setting feel bland. On the other hand, I find games like *Exalted*, *Warhammer Fantasy*, and *Castle Falkenstein* exceptionally flavorful, but hard to modify or extricate from their assumed setting. My personal sweet spot is a rules set that is easy to modify, nicely tailored to a specific genre, but not tied to any specific setting.

Here are some rules systems I commonly turn to when it's time to start world-building in various genres:

Cyberpunk	*Cyberpunk 2020* (R. Talsorian Games)
Hard Science Fiction	*Traveller* (GDW/Mongoose)
Heroic Fantasy	*Adventurer Conqueror King System* (Autarch)
Horror	*Call of Cthulhu* (Chaosium)
Mecha	*Mekton Zeta* (R. Talsorian Games)
Post Apocalyptic	*Barbarians of the Aftermath* (Jabberwocky Media)
Space Opera	*Hard Nova* (Precis Intermedia)
Superheroes	*Mutants & Masterminds* (Green Ronin)

If you are familiar with these games, you can probably identify why their mechanics support the genre. As already noted, *Cyberpunk 2020* has "live fast, die young" game mechanics loaded with crits and botches. It also has an almost fractal depth of technology and gear combined with a clever "humanity loss" mechanic, where cyberware slowly eats away your character's empathy as he becomes more machine than man.

Traveller gets the hard sci-fi nod for its career path system, which creates characters who feel like they are part of a high-tech society, not isolated wanderers in the post-apocalypse. The original game even suggests that the "game statistics" are part of a universal hexadecimal rating system actually employed in the galactic society the characters live in. My rating is UPP 677BA8.

The *D20 System* (which is the chassis for *Dungeons & Dragons*) is of course is an obvious choice because of its widespread popularity, but the popularity is not coincidental. By accident or not, *D&D's* class and level mechanics perfectly encapsulate the enduring myth of the hero's journey, wherein a youth is called to adventure and rises to greatness thereby. I used the D20 System as the basis for my own RPG, *Adventurer Conqueror King System*, which (as the name suggests) is all about those themes. (Don't underestimate the hero's journey: The reason most *D&D* campaigns tell the same story over and over is because it's the best story.)

Reasons of space preclude further annotation but each system above has similar implicit or explicit mechanics that support the genre. Consider these my recommendations as to systems, or if less charitably disposed, a disclosure of my biases.

CHAPTER 7

TOPS AND BOTTOMS

Having previously explored how the GM can best tackle the roles of judge, storyteller, and adversary, in the last chapter I introduced the role of worldbuilder, and discussed the need to choose your genre and rules setting before you start building your world.

Now we come to actual world-building. When it comes to world-building, there are two major schools of design that you need to know about: "top down" and "bottom up." Proponents of "top down" design are world-focused. They like to establish a framework for their world, laying out the backstory, major characters, and points of interest in advance. The player characters, when they are created, are made to fit the world. In this way, the gamemaster achieves a holistic creation, in which each part makes sense in the context of the whole.

Proponents of "bottom up" design are player-focused. They begin with whatever will be in the immediate vicinity of the player characters, and flesh that area out in great detail. They generally leave the framework of their world open, or at most very thinly sketched, feeling that major characters and points of interest can best be developed over the course of play. Often the "bottom up" GM will create sections of the world as needed to fit the needs of the player characters, or even let them be created by the players themselves. In this way, the gamemaster builds an open setting that is shaped to the needs and tastes of the players as they evolve in play.

Many early campaigns in the hobby began with bottom-up design. Gary Gygax's famous *Greyhawk* setting, for 1st edition *Dungeons & Dragons*, was a bottom-up design. Greyhawk began with a town (the city of Greyhawk), with a nearby dungeon (the castle of a mad wizard). The rest of the setting was fleshed out over time in increasing detail. The same is true of Dave Arneson's *Blackmoor* and Ed Greenwood's *Forgotten Realms*. In contrast, many modern campaigns are designed from the top-down. *Dark Sun*, *Eberron*, and *Dragonlance*, for instance, were all campaigns that began with a framework and backstory.

Which is better largely depends on your personal preferences, but there are some tonal factors to consider. Top-down design lends itself to high fantasy, in which the scope of the adventures is potentially epic. Bottom-up design lends itself to swords-and-sorcery, in which the adventures are of a more personal scope, and what matters most is the characters, not the world. Top-down design tends to result in a world that is flavored and thematic, but less flexible. If you don't write in a place for minotaurs into your top-down setting initially, they are hard to add later. In contrast, bottom-up-design worlds tend to be much more gonzo: Aztecs rub shoulders with Romans, and things tend to get added that don't fit into any larger pattern, because there isn't any. It's Frodo's Middle Earth v. Conan's Hyboria.

TOP-DOWN, ZOOM-IN

My personal design method falls in between the two schools. I call it "top-down, zoom-in." The "top-down, zoom-in" approach means starting with a light top-down framework, but creating increasing detail as you get closer to the areas of the setting that the players are most likely to interact with. Ideally, you end up with a setting that has much of the openness and playability of a bottom-up campaign, and much of the cohesiveness of a top-down setting.

Top-Down, Zoom-In starts with a one-paragraph "high concept" that establishes the setting, the flavor, and the overall scope of the challenges. Here is an example from the very first iteration of the Auran Empire campaign, which later became the basis for the *Adventurer Conqueror King System*:

> AURA, City of Dawn, founded on an island said to be at the center of the world, where the Light of Ammonar first blazed and rose into the sky. Its founders were kings and prophets touched by the gods. Imbued with gifts of power by their divine lineage, the founders built a city of marvels and an empire that spread across the known world. For centuries, Aura's high sorcery and disciplined legions have guarded the empire against the rising tides of darkness around it. But over time the lineage of old has thinned and the magical bloodlines have failed. With fewer men and women of power born every generation, the high sorceries are coming to an end. The great wonders of the city are dimming. Magic is slipping into oblivion. And terrible creatures of darkness are emerging in the empire. Will heroes arise who can restore the glory and the grandeur of the empire, or will the world plunge into an age of darkness one thousand years in the making?

After the high concept, the next step is to do a quick sketch of the game mega-setting, along with a one-page write up to accompany the map, covering the major regions, their cultures, allegiances, and wars. By "mega-setting," I mean an area that is larger in scope than the area the game will actually take place in. For fantasy games that is usually the "known world," but in other settings, the scope of the mega-setting is going to depend on your particular choices. For instance, in *Classic Traveller*, the standard mega-setting is the Imperium of Man, covering something like 10,000+ worlds. In *Coyote Trails*, a game of the Wild West, the mega-setting is the 1870s American frontier, a setting smaller than a single nation.

After establishing the mega-setting, the next step is to write a two page backstory to accompany it, with a timeline of major events. For a fantasy campaign, a good backstory needs to provide for the following historical periods: (a) recent history; (b) modern history; (c) classical history; (d) ancient history; and (e) forgotten history. Recent history is what's happened so recently that people are still talking about it - an invasion of orcs, or a discovery of gold in the hills. Modern history is the history of the dominant culture of your setting. Classical history is the history of the culture that directly led into the modern one. For instance, in a Dark Ages Europe setting, classical history would be the Roman civilization directly preceding the fall. Ancient history is the history of culture(s) prior to the Classical. Forgotten history is the secrets that no one living remembers. I generally do about a paragraph for each.

If you're working outside the fantasy genre, your backstory needs will differ. In a space opera campaign taking place on a prison planet in a galactic empire, you might structure the backstory as (a) galactic history, (b) quadrant history, (c) sector history, (d) planetary history, and (e) government history, putting each progressively local history in the context of what preceded it.

Exactly how you write up your backstory is, again, going to depend on your choices of genre and setting. For instance, if you're running *Call of Cthulhu* set in 1920s Europe, in a sense the backstory is already written. In that case, what you are writing are the counter-factuals of the setting: Archduke Ferdinand was assassinated by agents of Great Cthulhu who sought to bring about worldwide bloodshed. On the other hand, in a typical fantasy setting, you'll truly be spinning something out of whole cloth.

After the backstory is written, next turn to whatever the primary culture or region of the game is going to be, and write three pages about its culture. This material, along with mega-setting map and overview, and the recent and modern history, is ultimately going to be provided to the players for use in creating their characters, so I focus on things that people need to know to create characters: How people look and dress, what weapons and armor are used, what tools and technologies are available, how they get around, what their general state of knowledge and learning is, their religion and government, and any important cultural attitudes. Even if you're running a pseudo-historical campaign, it's worth taking the time to write this up. You would be surprised how many of your players won't actually know what firearms were available in the 1870s Old West, or whether or not women wore corsets in the 1920s, or what the standard kit was for a soldier in Vietnam.

At this point, it'll be time to turn to the micro-setting of the campaign. The "micro-setting" is the scope of the setting that the players will actually interact with. Again, the size of the micro-setting can vary widely from a city to an interplanetary region; it all depends on the genre, tech, and style of the game. In *Cyberpunk 2020*, the micro-setting is usually a particular city, such as Night City or Neo-Tokyo. In fantasy, the micro-setting is usually a kingdom or duchy, such as *Dragon Age's* Ferelden. In *Traveller*, the micro-setting is usually a sub-sector of space, covering a dozen or more star systems.

When it comes to the micro-setting, you're essentially going to follow something not too different than the steps you just followed for the mega-setting. You'll start with a one paragraph "area concept" describing the micro-setting. Here's my micro-setting area concept for my *Auran Empire* campaign mentioned earlier:

Straddling the 100 miles between the Empire and the Great Waste beyond, the Borderlands have been contested throughout recorded history and its landscape is littered with ancient fortresses and battlefields. The great fortress of Türos Orn was built a millennium ago, during the Empyrean War, on the shores of Lake Laman by the great warrior-king Valerian Bellësareus. East of the Krysivor River are 400-year old keeps and watchtowers built to watch the Dark Wall during the Beastman Wars, now reduced to ruin. In the remnants of the elder forests, elven keeps lost during the Argollëan War, two hundred years ago, lurk hidden under vine and leaf. Along the Mirmen River, doughty forts from the Krysean Wars of last century still face westward. And along the western bank of the Krysivor, newly constructed strongholds guard against renewed threats from the Waste. For the past fifteen years, waves of beastmen barbarians have invaded the Borderlands, many breaking through to raid and pillage the Empire. Each victory against the beastman has been won by a narrower margin, against larger numbers. Monsters continue to pour into the Empire, and the border forts grow increasingly isolated and out-matched. Travel has grown perilous, and the power structure of the Empire has begun decentralizing to local warlords and private armies.

The dates and references were, of course, drawn from the mega-setting backstory previously written. After the area concept, the next step is a sketch map of the setting, a one page write up of the geography covering the major terrain features and settlements, and a two-page outline of the recent history of the micro-setting.

Like the mega-setting information, this material should be largely information that can be shared with the players, and in fact at this point, you will have reached a good stopping point. You should have about 10 pages of material. Go through and remove anything secret or sensitive, and compile it into a document. This is your "Player Reference Guide," which is the starter packet you can give to your players to create characters for your new campaign. While they are busy doing that, you'll be starting work on your Gazetteer - which we'll discuss next chapter.

CHAPTER 8
Go Go Gazette

In the last chapter, we discussed setting creation using the technique of "top-down, zoom-in." Following those guidelines should leave you with about 10 pages of material, including a high concept for your setting, a world map, a historical timeline of contemporary to forgotten history, and a micro-setting within your world where play is going to happen. The micro-setting ranges in size from a city (in *Cyberpunk 2020*) to a kingdom (in *D&D*) to an interplanetary region (in *Classic Traveller*).

Now, the astute reader will have noticed that the micro-setting from "Tops and Bottoms" is exactly the same size as the sandbox that forms the basis of the story web described in "It's Not Your Story." No coincidence, of course, because they're the same thing! The goal of the top-down zoom-in method is to give you the coherent framework you need to plausibly populate your sandbox and build your story web. I call the detailed write-up of the sandbox and story web a "Gazetteer," in homage to the classic *Dungeons & Dragons Gazetteer* supplements such as *Principalities of Glantri* and *Orcs of Thar*. That's where we turn our attention now.

If you're running a fantasy campaign, the sandbox/micro-setting is going to be a frontier or unexplored wilderness. If you are playing *Classic Traveller*, it's going to be one or two sub-sectors of star systems. For *Call of Cthulhu*, it might be a map of London circa 1929, for *Cyberpunk 2020* a map of your home town in 2020. Since the dominant rules and favorite settings of most gamers are fantasy, I'll use that as illustrative for this chapter, but the same general principles apply to other settings.

START WITH STATIC

Start with a hex map, roughly 30 hexes by 40 hexes, where each hex is 6 miles wide (about 30 square miles). That gives you a region 43,200 square miles. To put that into historical terms, that's a region about the size of Greece, and thus if history is any guide, seems large enough to justify a distinct civilization with its own gods, heroes, and epic adventures. You can draw this map yourself, or use any of the widely available wilderness maps from supplements such as *Points of Light* or the *Wilderlands of High Fantasy*.

Within that map, you will place 45 static points of interest. One-third of these should be settlements, towns and castles of humans and demi-humans, while the other two-thirds (30) are dungeons, lairs, or special areas. Of the 30 dungeons/lairs, aim for 3 mega-dungeons each designed for about 6-10 sessions of play; 10 dungeons designed for 1-2 sessions of play; and 17 small lairs designed for a half-session of play, i.e. 1 encounter. Each point of interest in the sandbox initially gets a paragraph of description.

For the dungeons and mega-dungeons, you'll just describe the dungeon briefly, to be fleshed out later, but for the small lairs, you can cover everything you'll need to use it in play. For instance:

> *Hex #28 Lair of the Chimera* - A copse of giant acacia trees rises from the steppes here, and many wild sheep, gazelle, and other animals graze on the shrubbery and fruit and water at the nearby pond. They are preyed on by a pack of 2 Chimeras (as per Monster Manual) that live in a sinkhole near the oasis. In the sinkhole, amidst bones of dead, are a

leather satchel with 15 amethysts (100gp each) and 1 small diamond (1,000gp) and 2 torn sacks of gold (1,200gp total).

Note that you don't actually have to create all the points of interest yourself. In fact, doing so is an enormous time sink. What I recommend is to cobble together a few dozen of your favorite modules, lairs, and encounters from magazines, websites, and commercial products and adapt them to your setting, focusing on just a few special areas to spend your time. In my own *Auran Empire* campaign, I've adapted everything from TSR's classic modules *Keep on the Borderlands* and *In Search of the Unknown* to dozens of free *One Page Dungeons*.

Go Dynamic

At this point, your sandbox should have a density of about one point of interest every 6 hexes (36 miles), putting them roughly 2 days apart at historical travel speeds. With (30 x 40) 1,200 hexes in your sandbox, the vast majority of the sandbox is empty of static encounters. Some available settings, like Geoffrey McKinney's *Carcosa*, have actually filled up every hex of their sandbox with encounters, but I don't think that's necessarily the best use of your time, because it guarantees most encounters will go unused.

I recommend instead creating a chart of wandering encounters for each type of terrain on your map. Then, on the wandering encounter chart, for each encounter, specify a percentage chance (usually around 25%) that the encounter will actually be a "dynamic lair" encounter. Create each of these dynamic lairs in advance, similar to the static lairs above, with one or two encounters that will take about a half session to deal with. The only difference between the two is that the static points of interest are pre-placed while the dynamic points of interest are placed as the party travels around.

Here's an example of a simple dynamic point of interest:

> *Manticore Cistern*
> Lair: Mountain, 20%
> Map Location: _____
>
> An ancient Zaharan cistern has collapsed here, creating a
> sinkhole, 300' wide and 120' deep. The remnants of the
> fluted columns that once supported the cistern are visible,
> like jagged teeth rising up from the waterline, and small
> metal objects glitter below the water. The abandoned cistern
> is the lair of **four manticores**. 6,000gp in Zaharan coinage
> is scattered across the floor of the cistern, which is used as a
> lure by the manticores.

So, when in mountains, if the party encounters manticores randomly, there's a 20% chance they actually discovered a manticore lair in an ancient cistern. When discovered, I write down the hex number where it is located in case the party returns to the area. Sometimes the party stops to investigate and sometimes they don't. Each lair is unique and can only be discovered once, so for very common creatures (goblins, etc.) I create 2-3 lairs for each.

From the party's point of view, they cannot tell the difference between the pre-placed static lairs and the random lairs. It just seems like wherever they go, there is a mix of wandering encounters, lairs, and dungeons to be discovered. If they actually were to look at the sandbox map, though, what they would see is lots of empty hexes with unusually high clusters of monster lairs that happen to be along the routes they've traveled. (For maximum effect, tie the dynamic encounters into your story web, too.)

I think dynamic points of interest are such an important part of building a gazetteer that I wrote an entire book of them. It's called *Lairs & Encounters* and you can find it on DriveThruRPG and your favorite flagship gaming store. Or, if you sign up for my Autarch newsletter by sending an email to alex@autarch.co, I will send you a **free PDF copy** of the *Lairs & Encounters* supplement. I hope you'll take me up on the offer – it's a great supplement.

BALANCING THE CHALLENGE

In a few games, mostly science fiction, player characters are relatively static, but in most RPGs, characters advance from weak-kneed apprentices to mighty heroes and experts over the course of play. If that's the case, you need to take the reality of the leveling curve into account when creating your gazetteer.

The easiest way to handle it is to set your sandbox up as a borderlands environment because it gives you a built-in structure that explains the gradient of challenges the party faces. To build a borderlands, first put a string of border forts (or towns, space stations, etc.) running along one axis of the map, about 1/3 of the way in. To the rear of the border forts, put the main town/settlement. Beyond the border forts will be "the Wilderlands" or "the Waste" or whatnot, where the majority of the dungeons and lairs will lie. (Warning: Do NOT call this area "the Taint." Your players will never stop torturing you about it if you do. Learn from my mistakes.)

Place the lairs and dungeons such that the deeper the players travel into the wilderness, the more dangerous it becomes. Put a few areas of higher-than-normal danger close to the border but in geographically isolated or hidden places; for instance, an evil fortress high up on a mountain, or a very deep underground river, or behind a fiendishly clever secret door. Put your mega-dungeons such that one is close and pretty easy, one is a moderate distance away and relatively hard, and one is far, far away and murderously hard. Build your dynamic lairs and wandering encounters such that they are at a mid range of difficulty. For instance, in *Adventurer Conqueror King System* and similar games, the mid-range is 5th to 9th level.

The result of this structure is that early on in the campaign, the party hangs near the border forts. They can't risk the dangerous wandering encounters of the wilderness (which will be several levels higher than them) so they tend to travel from border fort to border fort, assisting each fort in clearing out whatever threats are nearby. Then when they reach a certain level of confidence, they begin to go into the wilderness, knowing they can handle any wandering encounters they run into. Again, they work from border fort to border fort, but this time in widening circles of exploration into the wilderness. As their power peaks, they will begin conducting forays deeper in the wilderness, far beyond the border forts, perhaps capturing or building strongholds to use as a staging point for deeper forays into harder challenges. The occasional high-level areas close to the border (like the castle on the mountain) serve as a reminder of the evil that lurks beyond, and also as a nice taste of what they can expect when they are ready to go deep.

Of course, if you're building a cyberpunk or science fiction setting, "borderlands," "border fort," and "wilderness" will take on radically different forms. For instance, in a cyberpunk setting where you play *Bladerunner* or *Judge Dredd* style cops, the "borderlands" might be the last city district under governmental control, the "border forts" might be fortified police precinct buildings, and the "wilderness" might be the combat zone beyond. In a science-fiction setting that's exploring strange new worlds where no man has gone before, the "borderlands" might be a neutral zone at the edge of Federation territory, the "border forts" would be star bases and colonies, and the "wilderness" would be the unexplored final frontier.

With a gazetteer complete, it's time to turn to techniques to transform your sandbox into a "world in motion" that lives and breathes. Read on…

FURTHER READING

In addition to my own *Adventurer Conqueror King System* and *Lairs & Encounters* supplement, I highly recommend the following books, blogs, and settings to any student of sandbox gamemastering.

- *Chrome Berets* by Thomas M. Kane (Atlas Games)

- *Classic Traveller Book 3 - Worlds and Adventures* (Game Designers Workshop)

- *How to Make a Fantasy Sandbox* by Rob Conley (Bat in the Attic Games)

- *Night City Sourcebook* by Mike Pondsmith (R. Talsorian Games)

- *Points of Light* by Rob Conley (Goodman Games)

- *Supplement V: Carcosa* by Geoffrey McKinney (LOTFP) (WARNING! Adult content)

- *Wilderlands of High Fantasy* by Bob Bledsaw (Judges Guild)

CHAPTER 9

WORLDS IN MOTION

In the last chapter, we discussed the detailed write-up of your campaign "Gazetteer," including your setting map, sandbox key, and story web. If you followed those guidelines, you've ended up with a gazetteer with about 40-50 static points of interest, including settlements, lairs, and dungeons, spread across a campaign map; and about 40-50 dynamic lairs to use for random encounters in empty areas.

At this point you have what one D&D blogger calls an extreme sandbox, in which the PCs can go anywhere and do anything. The world is essentially a very large dungeon and the points of interest are set-piece encounters or traps. The clues in your story web are like corridors that carry your party from one adventure to the next. If you just want to start running your campaign, you can actually stop world-building right here - it's a perfectly serviceable way to play. But if you want to engross yourself further, the next step is to put your world in motion.

A world in motion is one in which effects occur of which the players are not the purposeful or apparent cause. I say "purposeful or apparent" cause because, in many cases, the actions of the players will actually be the cause, through triggering, but this might be without their knowledge or intent. There are four basic techniques you can use to put your world in motion: triggered events, wandering NPCs, hand-crafted content, and random events.

SOMETIMES YOU FIND TROUBLE...

A trigger is an event that precipitates other events in your campaign world. Triggers are exceptionally common in videogames, and it's a safe bet that anyone who has played a computer RPG is quite familiar with them, so I won't belabor you with too much definition.

The key value of triggers is that they allow you to offer content that is time-sensitive. For instance, gladiatorial games are very interesting while they are occurring, much less so after they've occurred. One could include gladiatorial games with a trigger: "The first time the party visits the Imperial Capital, the town criers are announcing that the Great Games are to be held in three day's time. Gladiators are needed!"

A more advanced use of triggers is to have a trigger in one location set off results in other locations. For example, "The first time the party visits any village after the Summer Solstice they see proclamations announcing there will be Gladiatorial Games in the Imperial Capital in a fortnight."

Triggers can also be keyed against each other. Imagine that you place ancient calendar stones hidden in the wilderness that warn of the end times. At whatever point the party discovers the first calendar stone, the end times are set to 2 years away. If they later discover other calendar stones, they adjust based on what was first triggered, so that if it's been ten months since the first calendar stone was found, now the end times are fourteen months away. Other triggers placed within the setting can then be keyed to whether the end times are near, with encounters that change to include additional undead, more powerful magic, and so on.

The risk with using triggers is that sometimes the party can set off triggers on a timeline that is quite different than what you envisioned when you put the trigger in place. For instance, imagine that they stop into a village to have a companion magically healed, and sets off the "gladiator games" trigger. It's highly unlikely the party will stop its quest to go to the capital on short notice; if you trigger the event, it's going to be wasted. What to do in such a circumstance depends on your free time and your personal judgment.

If you have sufficient time and energy, you can allow the event to be "wasted" and write up what happened in the party's absence; this will let them know that the world really does go on without them, and that there is an opportunity cost to each decision. Alternatively you can delay the trigger until they've finished the quest, or modify it on the fly to extend the time available to give them a real chance to follow up. Remember, as always, that your goal is to offer the players meaningful choices.

SOMETIMES TROUBLE FINDS YOU

The second technique for putting your world in motion is to place some of your major static NPCs into the wandering encounter charts for the setting. The exact nature and reason for the NPC's presence on the wandering chart should be kept loosely defined, because if and when these encounters occur, you will interpret the NPC's reasons for appearing and behavior upon appearance in light of the party's past deeds. As the *Book of Five Rings* says, "It is very difficult to understand this merely by reading, but you will soon understand with a little practice." As an example, in my campaign, an ancient green dragon ruled the humanoids of the Istrith Forest. The party had been leading a band of mercenaries to attack the humanoids. While the mercenary band was camped out, the party had the misfortune of suffering a random encounter with the ancient green dragon. I interpreted this to mean that the dragon from the nearby dungeon had roused itself to deal with the raiders in its territory, and staged the encounter as an attack on the party's campsite! This was pretty brutal, and they lost several characters and most of their mercenary band (50+) before the dragon used up its breath weapons and left.

The "wandering NPC" system gives a sense that the enemy can strike back but it avoids you having to run the campaign as a wargame where you actually work out every detail of the NPCs' moves. They are off "doing other stuff" unless a random encounter says otherwise, but when a random encounter says so, you can interpret the results as smartly as possible.

GETTING (HAND) CRAFTY

That said, there are occasions when you should work out every detail of a particular NPCs' moves. If the party's deeds place them in active confrontation with a major antagonist, it makes sense to develop some hand-crafted content in response to the party's actions. I generally do this in perhaps one out four sessions, mostly when I think the party is trying to "game" the system, i.e. acting in ways that only make sense if you assume the NPCs are static and stupid. You need to hand-craft enough content in response to their deeds to persuade the party that they are better off assuming the entire world is a smoothly running simulation and every NPC is fully fleshed out and intelligent. A simple example from my home campaign should suffice to illustrate: The party poked a red dragon's nest and then ran back to town without killing the dragon, so I ruled that the dragon followed them back and attempted to burn the town to the ground.

THE ORACULAR POWER OF DICE

The final technique, random events, is a beloved mainstay of old school gaming. Random events are similar to wandering monsters, but whereas a wandering monster is usually a simple fight-and-forget encounter, random events can be used as seeds to deepen the campaign experience. The key is to interpret the random event in the context of what's come before it. This is, again, something of an art that comes from practice. In my Auran Empire campaign, I used a set of charts available in the Judges Guild

Ready Reference guide that included town crier rumors, proclamations, boons and duties, and so on. Whenever the party loitered in a settlement, I rolled on these charts, and then interpreted the results according to things that are going on in the game. Sometimes this led to a quick battle - such as a "call to arms - town is under attack" result that I interpreted to be a counter-attack by an orc tribe the party had recently raided. Occasionally these random events triggered an entire session's worth of play, such as when a "pestilence" event led the party's cleric to travel from town to town trying to stop an outbreak of the Black Death.

Some of you will no doubt ask, of course, "Why can't you just have all this occur as a result of GM fiat?" In other words, why can't the gamemaster just hand craft when and where all events occur using his best judgment, rather than rely on triggers and random encounters at all? The most lucid answer to this question comes from James Maliszewski. His detailed answer – "the Oracular Power of Dice" – is that the embrace of events beyond your control is an integral part of the gaming experience for the GM Roll the dice. Chapter 17 discusses the oracular power of dice in more detail.

CHAPTER 10
HOW TO HOST AN RPG SESSION

If you've followed the advice in the preceding chapters, you've learned how to be a judge, an adversary, a storyteller, and a worldbuilder. Maybe you've even crafted your own world. Now it's time to actually sit down and run an RPG session.

Running an RPG session, especially your first time, is hard, and a first-time gamemaster can quickly make a mess of things. On the other hand, a well-practiced and experienced gamemaster can make hosting an RPG session seem easy; he or she knows all the secrets for gathering folks, getting them in the head space to game, and then running them through. Let's talk about what those secrets are.

WHEN AND WHERE

One of the first challenges you face in deciding to host an RPG session is determining when and how long you'll play. I generally have had the most success in getting groups to play on Mondays or Thursdays. The specific day is going to depend on your and their schedules, of course, but by avoiding the precious weekend nights you take a lot of pressure off the participants. Mondays, in particular, have worked out well as they give the weekend beforehand for campaign preparation, if needed.

After years of trying various patterns of play, I've found that a four- to five-hour session length is optimal. Four to five hours is, not coincidentally, about the length of dinner and a movie, a tailgate plus football game, or a concert plus drinks. If you play after work, it means you can play at 7pm and wrap up before midnight, which fits comfortably into most people's after-work schedules.

For venue, a quiet room with comfortable seating and a large table is ideal. I've found the best choice is the gamemaster's home, provided he has a large enough table or living room. Of course, if one of the players has a dedicated game room where you can have rules and miniatures spread out, go with that. I generally avoid trying to run games in public places such as game stores or coffee shops, because it's loud and uncontrolled, which makes it hard for introverts to feel immersed and comfortable. That said, if you have a villainous roommate or live in a Tokyo sleep-coffin, it might be your best option. Whatever you choose, it's best to find one venue for your campaign and stick with it. You can try to make a rotating venue (one in which each player hosts for a week, for instance) work, but I guarantee that the "friction of war" will frequently cause tardy and lost players who end up at the wrong location.

REWARDING REFRESHMENTS

Role-playing games are best enjoyed with food and drink. Every party's taste in refreshments will vary, of course, ranging from the traditional Mountain Dew and chips to fruit smoothies and diced vegetables, but your party can't be expected to defeat the dark lord on an empty stomach. Nor, for that matter, can you speak for five hours on a parched throat.

I've found a simple technique to always ensure there's a large and varied supply of food and drink at each gaming session: I offer bonus experience points to players that bring munchies. This works in every campaign. In my *Classic Dungeons & Dragons* campaign, I offered a 5% bonus on experience points earned in the session; in my *Mutants & Masterminds* campaign, I offered 1 extra Hero Point; and in *Cyberpunk 2020* it was 10 bonus improvement points. To kick things off, you can even offer an additional bonus (+5% more) to whoever brings the best array of refreshments. It rewards pro-social behavior and encourages everyone to chip in.

One important note on refreshments: Beware the drunken gamer. Whether the party is attempting to role-play or devise battle tactics, a drunkard gets in the way and ruins the experience of the other players. While we keep beer on hand, we also maintain a hard and fast rule at our campaigns that anyone who gets drunk is ejected from play. We save our serious drinking for beer-and-pretzels board games, or visits to the local inns and taverns.

Running the Session

With a half-dozen or so friends gathered around the table, gossip and small talk is a certainty. The players can easily chat away for hours and then complain that they didn't have enough time to play. It can seem rude or intimidating to interrupt everyone and demand their attention on Your Game, but that's your job as GM. I like to give everyone about 10 minutes to get settled, and then start the game. I find that having a routine to open each session really helps send the signal that it's time to get started.

In my campaigns, I usually open each session by playing some epic trailer music and giving a short recap of the prior session. The recap reminds everyone of what went on the last time we all gathered, and usually prompts roars of laughter, a lot of "oh that's right," and pledges of renewed vengeance or greed. After that, I quickly describe where the party is, and ask them what they want to do.

This technique, of describing the scene and then asking the players what they want to do, is one of the main tools in any gamemaster's arsenal for maintaining the pace of the game. Plan to use it frequently over the next few hours. Anytime the players get bogged down arguing for more than 10-15 minutes, or seem like they are at a loss as to how to proceed, give them an updated summary of the situation at hand and ask them for their actions. It will usually trigger them to do *something*. Be sure to mention how long it's been since the last update you provided, what people are currently doing, any objects they haven't yet explored, and offer some sense that time is running out.

For example, consider the following description, offered to a party that isn't sure what to do next: "OK, so you've been standing in the vampire's tomb arguing in hushed whispers for the past ten minutes, unsure what to do. Viktir is lurking in the corner, while Marcus is eyeballing the exit. The black curtain still hangs across the south wall, covered with dust and cobwebs, untouched in centuries. In the distance you can now hear low groaning." The party might decide to head for the exit, or check out the curtain, or get ready to fight whatever is groaning, but they'll do something.

After about four hours of play, it'll be time to wind the session down. When the session ends, if the party isn't in a safe area, be sure to record how much damage (or equivalent) they've suffered, what spells or mana they've expended, and other notes on their condition - players are not very incentivized to remember that, after all!

If possible, it's courteous to maintain your scheduled duration as a hard deadline. The major exception to this rule is that you should try never to end a session in the middle of a fight - Not only is it bad for immersion, it's quite hard to keep track of the tactical details after a week. The ideal way to end the session is after a hard fight or dramatic encounter, about

10-15 minutes before everyone needs to head out. After a good game, there's usually an enjoyable "post game recap" where people discuss what happened. It's fun to review your own game, and it'll provide valuable insight to you as to what people most liked and disliked in the session.

With that, we've covered the basics! In the chapters ahead, we'll move into more advanced topics: managing problems and players, running long-term campaigns, and other techniques for the expert gamemaster.

CHAPTER 11

MANAGING PROBLEMS AND PLAYERS

Once you start running role-playing games, you will likely, sooner rather than later, see a shouting match develop. It could be between you and one of your players; more likely it will be between two players. If you're lucky, it'll be at least thinly-veiled as in character; if you're not lucky, it will involve a messy break-up over when he cheated on her with the elf paladin, or worse.

Role-playing games can be emotionally charged, and unlike videogames, there isn't the filter of a monitor and gamepad between us and the other player. What happens is in your face. As the GM of the game, you'll be the person who assembled the group, and one of the signs of a great gamemaster is the ability to manage and control social problems within the group you've assembled. Even better is to prevent them from ever occurring.

It's time to step away from the world of your imagination and turn to a messier world: The world of problem players, personality conflicts, and social pitfalls.

PLAYER VERSUS PLAYER

Many, though not all, problems in role-playing game campaigns arise when one or more of the players is out of step with the overall social dynamic of the rest of the players. I have seen three basic social dynamics in which players interact in a tabletop campaign: Collective, Competitive-Collective, and Individualist. Each of these social styles has its own implicit rules that govern how the players behave towards each other.

The Collective play style is characterized by a "one for all, all for one" mentality. Each of the players subsumes his individual play into the greater good of the campaign. In a Collective campaign, the implicit rules are: (1) each player will create a character that fits into and gets along well with the collective; (2) each player is entitled to a chance to enjoy the campaign simply by virtue of being a fellow player; and (3) the collective as a whole will democratically make major campaign decisions, and all the players will abide by them.

The Competitive-Collective play style might be summarized as "we're in this together, but I don't have to like it." In the Competitive-Collective campaign, the group has implicitly agreed to the following: (1) no player will create a character that cannot fit into the collective, though they need not be friendly to each other; (2) no player is entitled to enjoy the campaign except by virtue of his character; and (3) the collective as a whole will democratically make major campaign decisions, and all the players will abide by them.

The Individualist play style might be summarized as "all against all" or "every man for himself." Here the implicit rules are: (1) each player makes his own character and decisions and accepts the consequences; (2) no player will get angry out of game at another player for the actions of their respective characters; and (3) major campaign decisions will be made based solely on what the characters decide in the game.

Sometimes the social dynamic simply evolves out of a particular rules set or campaign theme, or out of years of playing with the same group.

Other times the group agrees in advance. Opinions will vary widely as to which of these social dynamics is the best. I have played with all of them at various times and it can put an interesting spin to try the same game different ways. *Cyberpunk 2020* with an Individualist style is a game of treachery and betrayal; the same rules set with a Collective style is a game of a band of brothers in a dark world.

Regardless of what your group's social dynamic ends up being, social problems occur when part of the group is out of sync with the whole. What follows are some common examples of problems.

DEAD AND BACK AGAIN

If you've followed my advice regarding the agency theory of fun then character death is bound to happen sooner or later. As a gamemaster, I believe that when character death occurs, it's your responsibility to introduce the player's new character into the game as quickly and seamlessly as possible. In *D&D*, the classic way to handle this is to introduce the new character as a prisoner found left for dead in one of the next few rooms (often with a suspiciously similar class and name ...). It's quick and it works.

But sometimes, when the surviving characters find the new player character, they decide not to let him into the party. What do you do as GM now? It will totally depend on the social dynamic of your campaign.

In a Collective campaign, you need to remind the players that the new character should expect to be admitted readily and probably given some gear and assistance to get into play swiftly. In most Collective campaigns, the players have created heroic, good-intentioned characters, so this is not too much of a stretch. But even if their characters are world-weary cynics with deep suspicions about the world, in a Collective game the players agreed to put the group ahead of the individual, and agreed that each player is entitled to participate, so the need to introduce and integrate their fellow player should trump the particulars of in-character behavior. If the majority of the players have a problem with this, then you probably don't actually have a Collective campaign!

In a Competitive-Cooperative campaign, you need to remind the players that the new character should expect to be admitted, but probably not warmly; the player can expect his new character to get lots of in-character questioning or wisecracks and a "show me what you can do" attitude. Still, it should be a given that ultimately he'll be admitted to the party and play will go on.

In a true Individualist campaign, you don't need to do anything. Here the new character had better hope he's been created with knowledge, skills, or other utility to his prospective comrades, as the players are not beholden by any social contract to be nice to him. It might turn out that the party refuses to take the new character along. In response, he might follow them to aid them and prove his worth by backstabbing them during their next fight! Of course, if they fear backstabbing, the characters might kill their erstwhile comrade.

THAT'S WHAT MY CHARACTER WOULD DO!

Imagine that a player's old character has died, and a new character has been introduced into the group, as discussed above. Unbeknownst to his new party members, however, this new character holds a radically different moral code or alignment than his new comrades. During the party's next engagement, he ruthlessly betrays them, leading to the death of the entire party. "Why did you do that?" you ask. "That's what my character would do!" says the traitor. What do you do as GM in this circumstance?

If this happens in a Collective campaign, then there's been a violation of all of the implicit rules of the campaign. First, the player introduced a character who didn't fit into the collective. Second, by purposefully getting everyone killed, the player didn't respect the other players' right to enjoy the game. And third, by purposefully causing the campaign to end, the player breached the agreement to democratically decide major campaign decisions. You should stop the game, pull the offending player aside, explain that his behavior is out of bounds for this campaign, and rewind. A continuously problematic player should be ejected.

If this happens in a Competitive-Collective campaign, there's still been a violation of the social dynamic, because the player introduced a character who didn't fit into the collective and because he purposefully caused the campaign to end unilaterally. That said, since this game is partly Competitive, and there's a strong argument that you ought not intervene with GM fiat. I think the best way to handle this situation is to have a quick player vote - rewind events or let them stand.

If this happens in an Individualist campaign, then it's possible that nothing wrong has happened. The party wasn't required to take in the new player character, and characters aren't required to be nice to each other. As GM, your responsibility is to remind the betrayed players that this is the sort of game they're playing and they agreed not to get angry out of game. However, it's also possible that the traitor has just gone out of his way to purposefully wreck the fun, not because of what his character would do, but to get back at the party that let him die. Resolving this can get complex!

My general rule when addressing the solution to the "TWMCWD" problem is that *it doesn't matter whether the problem behavior is "actually" what the character would do*. It doesn't matter whether the player is a consummate role-player playing a black-hearted villain, or just a jerk. All that should matter is whether it's a problem.

In a Collective campaign, there's an implicit agreement to create characters that are "one for all, all for one," so if a player makes a character who is a sociopathic traitor, he has created the problem. If he purposefully chooses to role-play a jerk when everyone else has agreed to role-play nice people that means... he's choosing to be a jerk. And the better he is at role-playing, the more of a jerk he chooses to be. If you're running a Collective campaign, you don't want jerks. Whether they are actually jerks or pretending to be jerks doesn't matter at all.

On the other end of the spectrum, in an Individualist campaign, the players have implicitly agreed that it's "every man for himself," and that they won't let treachery in game make them angry out of game. But if one player behaves in such a way as to make it impossible for the other players to not be angry, then he has created the problem. For instance, imagine that in the last six campaigns, a hypothetical player named Bob has always played a sociopathic thug who always tries to kill the party when they are weak. In the seventh campaign, the party members can hardly be blamed for murdering all of Bob's characters on sight. Bob might be "in character" in his treachery, and the party members acting totally out of character in dispatching them, yet it's Bob who is the problem.

PLAYER VERSUS GAMEMASTER

Anyone who has ever watched a baseball player shout at an umpire over a bad call is familiar with the love-hate relationship that players have with their pastime's referees. The same is true of role-playing game players and their relationship with their gamemasters. There will be times that players can get very... *rowdy*... with their GM over a particular ruling, encounter, or choice. And, as between us gamemasters, there are times when you might have some sore feelings towards your players. At some point, someone will check Twitter while you are relaying information that warns of a trap ahead, then bitch at you when their character walks into said trap and dies. It's hard not to be annoyed (try to remember, they're only upset because they care).

But such happenings are minor and if you are following the guidelines in this book – not railroading your players, making clear and fair rulings, playing honestly with the adversaries, and so on – then they are unlikely to derail your play. Sometimes, however, more serious issues can arise between you and one or more players, and these can be some of the most uncomfortable challenges for any GM.

THEME PARK ATTENDEES

Imagine if you were allowed to choose between two vacations: a safari in Africa or a trip to Disney's Animal Kingdom. An actual safari involves vaccinations, mosquitos, tents, jet lag, and the risk of being eaten by lions or rabid gazelles. A trip to Disney's Animal Kingdom involves luxury hotels with air conditioning and a carefully-controlled experience designed to give great memories. A lot of people are going to choose the theme park.

Similarly, some players don't want an RPG world in motion with real risk. They want a theme park RPG. Now, it is my considered judgment that these players are missing out. I believe that participating in an agent-focused sandbox campaign is the most fun a player can have in a role-playing game. There are other hobbies that can afford a better theme park experience. MMORPGs, for instance, that eschew permanent character death and allow infinite chances to succeed at quests and stories, are ideal platforms for theme park play. Only the tabletop RPG can offer agency-centered sandbox play. And that's why the advice in this book is all about creating a living, breathing world-in-motion that empowers yours players with the agency to make real choices in the game.

But I am not the exclusive arbiter of fun on Planet Earth, and many people find joy in things I find boring – golf, gardening, and scrapbooking come to mind. Conversely, many people don't take pleasure in things I enjoy, like military history, spreadsheets, or sandbox campaigns. And there is a downside to my style of campaign. With real choice comes real risk of loss – of loot, of XP, of henchmen, of a character. Some players simply don't want that. They want the theme park, not the safari.

If you have one or more players like this, you'll find out the first time your group experiences a terrible setback – when a beloved character dies, or the party fails to achieve an important quest. They will let you know in no uncertain terms that they are not interested in losing, did not sign up to be killed, and cannot believe you didn't run the game in such a way as to make sure such tragedy didn't ensue.

SO WHAT DO YOU DO?

If you and the majority of your other players are enjoying the campaign, I think the right thing to do is to be honest with the upset players: Say that you aren't running a theme park, don't intend to run a theme park, think a sandbox is a better way to play, and ask them to give it a chance. They might grow to like it.

But sometimes they won't want to give it a chance, and sometimes they will give it a chance and still not like it. When that happens, the best thing to do is probably to ask the upset players to leave the campaign. If they stay in the campaign, it often creates bad blood. I've seen friendships end over events in games, and it's never worth it. It's better to just agree to disagree about what you want out of your RPG hobby.

Now, it could also be the case that most or even all of your group may decide they'd rather visit a theme park then play in a world in motion. If **everybody** wants a theme park, a rollercoaster, and a railroad, and you're offering a safari, a sandbox, and a story web, you have a serious problem.

So then what? Well, if it were me, I'd step down and let someone else GM. I don't enjoy running those types of RPG campaigns and I'd be bad at it. If my style weren't to the group's taste, it'd be better to let someone else run the show. But you can always change your GM style and give your players what they want. This book won't help you as much, but there's no statute on how to have fun. It's what you make of it.

THE POLITICIZATION OF GAMING

The reality of 21st century America is that virtually everything has been politicized. Turn on ESPN, and it's politics. Read your FB feed, and it's politics. And, lately, it has spilled into gaming in a big way. It's become common for political discussions to arise over tropes in RPGs that have been around for decades. When I started gaming in 1979, no one ever worried about whether Conan was an example of toxic masculinity. When I ran Cyberpunk 2020 in the 1990s, no one really cared whether it was a critique of turbo-capitalism. It's different nowadays.

I am not going to say that politicization is a good thing or a bad thing. There are lots of people who believe that everything ought to be made political, because allowing things to be apolitical is itself a political choice to support the status quo. Conversely, there are lots of people who believe that escapist entertainment that avoids politics can be healthy and heal divides between people of different opinions.

What I am going to say is that politicization is a **big thing**, and you have to decide how to handle it for your campaign. There are two distinct areas to concern yourself with and a few strategies to take for each.

The first area is discussion of real-world politics at the gaming table. Your options here are to ban it or permit it. I tend to take the view that it's better to ban it for the same reason that polite dinner conversation used to exclude politics and religion. Politics tends to be an emotional topic and if players are from different political tribes, a single partisan comment can quickly spark an argument that can derail play and cause bad feelings all around.

Even if everyone in the gaming group shares the same political views, it's not clear it makes the experience of playing an RPG better to talk about it. In today's media-saturated world, political headlines hit us 24/7 on our smart phones and social feeds. It can be really freeing to get away from that, whatever your beliefs, and just play the game. And it's a lot easier to immerse yourself in a fantasy world when you're not thinking about the impact of tariffs on global trade.

Now, to be clear, I feel the same way about table talk about pretty much anything unrelated to RPGs, especially if it's a topic people get really partisan about. I don't want players spending game time chatting about the latest UNC vs. Duke basketball game, or Star Trek vs. Star Wars, either. That said, if you and your players are all like-minded politically and you want to talk politics, go for it. Again, there's no statute on how to have fun.

The second area is discussion of politics that arises from actions in the game. Let me given an example of what I mean. Imagine you are running an RPG in which the player characters are mercenaries in ancient Rome. In that era, it was altogether customary (indeed, considered downright merciful) to enslave captured prisoners-of-war. So it's entirely plausible, in the context of the game, for an NPC to hire the player characters to round up a gaggle of prisoners and escort them to the slave markets. But it's entirely possible a player might balk at this, not because of anything related to role-playing, but simply because real-world slavery is evil.

Or, imagine that you are running a game of *Cyberpunk 2020* in which the PCs are hitmen for the Night City Mafia. It's entirely plausible in-world they might get asked to assassinate a series of Yakuza leaders in Japantown in order to help the Mafia seize power. But a player might well find that distasteful or unacceptable, perhaps because it's cold-blooded murder or perhaps because of the racial aspect.

This sort of situation is a lot trickier to handle – you can't handle it by simply banning it, because the discussions will arise inevitably from in-game activity. There are three basic strategies. Because I like to make up jargon, I will call them the Historicist strategy, the Presentist strategy, and the Bespoke strategy.

The Historicist strategy holds that the player characters should act according to the game world's moral values, not their own. In a Historicist campaign set in ancient Rome, the PCs would be expected to role-play as if they viewed the world the way people of that era viewed it. They'd simply escort the prisoners to the slave markets and that would be that. In a Historicist campaign based on the Night City mob, the PCs would be expected to role-play as sociopathic mobsters. In short, your players are exploring how people very different than themselves lived and thought. That can be really freeing to some, and really upsetting to others.

The Presentist strategy holds that the player characters should carry the players' real-world moral values into the campaign and the GM should take that into account when running the game. So, for instance, in a

Presentist campaign set in ancient Rome, the PCs will have the same attitudes towards slavery that their players do – presumably as contemporary Westerners this will be one of loathing and contempt. In turn, it's your responsibility as GM to set up a world and story web that allows the player characters to act on their attitude. For instance, give them the chance to join Spartacus's slave revolt, or to start their own. In a Presentist campaign, your players are exploring how people like themselves would behave in a world with different moral and political structures.

Finally, the Bespoke strategy holds that the GM should build the players' real-world moral values into the fabric of the campaign world itself, hand-tailoring the world to the players' sensibilities. For instance, in an RPG set in ancient Rome, the GM might downplay the role of slavery in the world, so it only occurs "off camera", or even replace it with serfdom or indenture. Or the GM might simply not set the game in ancient Rome at all, but in some alternative world that has centurions and Caesars but not slaves. In our *Cyberpunk 2020* example, the GM might make up all new organized criminal gangs that are fictional and multicultural, without any of the ethnic ties that currently are associated with certain syndicates. In a Bespoke campaign, your players can feel comfortable exploring a world with familiar moral and particular structures.

There are pros and cons to each approach. The Historicist strategy affords the widest opportunity for role-playing experiences in worlds quite unlike our own. But most of humanity's history and lots of fictional human futures feature cultures with political and moral values that were downright awful. Adopting the Historicist strategy can mean your players are playing villains by today's standards.

The Bespoke strategy can make it easier to avoid unsettling topics, but it can also make it impossible to explore certain worlds or role-play certain characters in their original format. Middle-earth is grounded in J.R.R.

Tolkien's conservative Catholicism, and role-playing Aragorn in a Bespoke Middle-earth where God-given kingship and nobility by blood are pernicious would change the plot of *Lord of the Rings* by more than a little.

The Presentist strategy is perhaps the middle ground between the two, which can be appealing to many players. But the Presentist strategy can lead to a certain straightjacketing of the set of choices available. The players may feel morally obligated to "do something" about injustice in the game world.

Which strategy to adopt is very much a choice that needs to be particular to your gaming group. It's something you should talk about in advance of the campaign and agree to with your players. If it turns out that your players have widely different opinions on the matter, it's better to find out before you launch the campaign. It may well be that some players may be incompatible with the strategy you'd like to adopt, or with each other for any given strategy.

CHAPTER 12

THE CHALLENGE OF CAMPAIGNING

In Chapter 10 we reviewed the basics of running an RPG session, and last chapter we talked about the social dynamics of players and the problems that occur when one player is out of step with the rest of the group. In this Chapter, we're going to discuss how to sustain a successful long-term RPG campaign.

Running a long-term RPG campaign is the hallmark of the best gamemasters. The greatest long-term campaigns - *Greyhawk, Blackmoor, Glorantha, Forgotten Realms, Arduin, Wilderlands* - ran for decades, and literally changed the way people thought about fantasy and gaming. Such hallowed success is probably beyond us all these days, but running a long-term campaign is nevertheless an admirable goal and a wonderful experience.

I define a successful long-term RPG campaign as a campaign that runs on a regular schedule that allows the players to complete the experience available to them from that game. That could mean advancing from level 1 to 20; that could mean exploring the complete sandbox the GM has built; that could mean defeating a major villain. What it does not mean is a slow death because of lack of interest and involvement. And yet that's the fate of most campaigns. It doesn't need to be that way!

SCHEDULING FOR SUCCESS

The first step towards running a successful campaign is scheduling for success. During the halcyon days of *Greyhawk*, Gary Gygax ran his campaign six days out of seven, and he was writing not just the campaign, but all the rules, spells, and content! I am not as hardcore as Gary, but I am a firm believer that the most sustainable schedule for an RPG campaign is weekly, and at a minimum bi-weekly. Successful RPG campaigns are sustained by commitment - by the sense that "it's all real" - and that requires ongoing reinforcement of the activities. Campaigns are similar to TV shows in that they require an ongoing immersion in an imaginary world. Two weeks seems to be about the longest length of time most people can be away from their imaginary worlds without losing track of what's going on. One week keeps it fresh in their mind.

The single biggest obstacle towards running RPGs on a weekly basis is the false belief that maintaining a weekly game is impossible in today's world because we are all "too busy." But most of us are not, in fact, too busy. The real reason we seem too busy is because we have more options for things to do. After all, we live in the future! And in the future people have access to mobile phones, on-demand movies, endless videogames, non-stop social media, and more.

Consider that the average casual videogamer is now playing for 20 hours per week - or that the average person watches more than 33 hours of TV per week. Consider that a dedicated World of Warcraft gamer who raids twice per week and grinds the other nights spends 40 hours per week in his game. Consider the time spent by dedicated golfers, who may hit the course every weekend; or by ESPN enthusiasts, who watch sports daily plus all day Sunday as a major social gathering.

In contrast to these 20-to-40 hour commitments, running a successful RPG campaign takes just 5 hours once per week plus about 8-10 hours of prep time by the GM. Any of the hobbyists above have more than enough leisure time to run a weekly RPG campaign. If you're like most people, the real question is not "do I have time?", its really "is this actually one of the things I want to make a priority to do with my time?"

If the answer is yes, read on. If the answer is no, then you are better off running casual one-off sessions then attempting a major campaign. That's your choice.

How Many Players?

How many players should you invite to your weekly campaign? Sadly, gamemasters are unevenly distributed, and as a result some gamemasters struggle to find even one or two players while others run the "only game in town" and have to actively limit their players to a manageable number. Acknowledging that reality, there is still a definite sweet spot for how many players you should aim for: three to seven, with five being ideal.

Why is five players the ideal number? With five players, you have enough to cover all the common roles or classes in any game, without so many players that there's duplication. You can give each player sufficient in-game attention without slowing the game down. If one or even two players can't make a particular session, you can still run with a group of three or more. And in terms of seating, most dinner tables have six seats, meaning there's one for you and five for them.

If you are one of the lucky gamemasters who has access to a wide pool of players, you can certainly run with seven (I do), though it will slow the game down a bit. If you have more than seven, though, it's better if you can split them up into two groups, or get another gamemaster to help you out.

TABLETOP CAMPAIGNS ARE TEAM SPORTS, NOT SOCIAL EVENTS

If you're planning to start a successful campaign, you need to explain to your friends that you are not hosting a series of social events. You are starting an intramural sports team and asking them if they'd like to be on the team.

It's true that role-playing games are like social events in that much of the fun is socializing with your friends. But the problem with treating an RPG as a social event is that the etiquette of social events does not lend itself to RPGs at all. Consider the notion of "fashionably late" at a social event - where you demonstrate your social status by not bothering to show up until the event is already underway. Or consider the notion of "stopping by" a social event, where you put two-three events on the schedule and visit each one for only a portion of the time. Or even consider "blowing off" a social event, where you simply don't attend because something better came up. You can throw a party for guests who behave that way, but you sure can't run an RPG when the players are fashionably late, stopping by, or blowing it off.

That's why I recommend you position joining the campaign as akin to joining a sports team. People can often have trouble understanding why they need to show up on time and stay through until the end at a social event, but everyone understands that the quarterback needs to show up at the football game and finish all four quarters.

Moreover, many – if not most – people have been on an intramural sports team at one point in their life. That makes it a simple analogy for them to understand and puts into perspective the time commitment. A player who balks at committing to your campaign as an intramural sport is almost certainly a player who will miss a lot of sessions. And that's important, because missing sessions is one of the worst things a player can do to a campaign.

MISSING IN ACTION

Even with the most well-intentioned and dedicated players, there will be times when one or more of them can't make it. An ongoing challenge for every gamemaster is what to do when one or more players go "missing in action." I have seen recommendations ranging from cancelling the game to running with the missing player's characters killed and everything seen in between. Most of these recommendations are wrong.

The first thing to know is: Don't cancel the game. The game must go on. As long as you have more than half of your group available (3 players out of 5, for instance), the game goes on. Pragmatically, in any regular weekly campaign, there will almost certainly be one or two absent players in any given session due to work, illness, travel, kids, etc. If you cancel whenever one or two people are missing, then you'll be canceling more often than you are running. Philosophically, the campaign should be larger than any one player or any one faction of players. If you cancel because of someone else's decision that they can't or won't come play, then you've handed over control of the destiny of your campaign to that person.

There's no hard and fast rule about what you should do with the missing players' characters. It will depend on the style of game you are running. If you're running a collective group, then let the attending players run their friends' PCs and give everyone full experience points, so they stay on the same advancement curve. If you're running a competitive-collective group, then you should treat the missing player characters as NPCs, and award them a limited experience award. If you're running an individualist group, then the missing player characters are absent pursuing other agendas (or present as NPCs if that's impossible), and they should not get any experience.

I have used these methods in practice and they work very well. For instance, in our weekly (collective) ACKS campaign, with 7 players, we play if there are 4 players available. The attending players run the missing players' characters while they are away. When I ran an individualist Cyberpunk campaign, missing players were assumed to be off doing another mission. This sometimes resulted in them missing out on important decisions or fantastic wealth, but that's life in the dark future...

You Must Lead By Example

None of the advice above will sustain a campaign alone. You must sustain it. As gamemaster, you are the heart and soul of the group. If you show up late, you cannot expect the players to show up on time. If you do not invest time prepping for the game between sessions, you cannot expect the players to bother to remember what went on last session. If you cancel the game because you have a tummy ache, then you can't expect your players to have any more commitment.

But if you do have the commitment, running a long-term campaign is one of the most satisfying experiences you can enjoy. To paraphrase Sergeant Apone in Aliens, "Every pizza slice is a banquet! Every play session a parade! I love the campaign!"

CHAPTER 13

JUDGMENT DAY AFTER DAY

Last chapter, we talked about how to sustain a successful long-term RPG campaign, covering scheduling, party size, prioritization, and leadership. In this chapter, we turn our attention to the role of legal precedent in sustaining a long-running campaign.

Before I dive too much into the overlap of law and gaming, let me share two personal anecdotes. The first is that I got into law school, way back in 1997, after sending the admissions committee a set of game rules I had published. The committee was, I assume, impressed by my ability to formulate a set of rules that would guide behavior, as that is, after all, the essence of law. The second is that my law school third-year paper, published in 1999, was an argument that game designs are functionally the law of massively multiplayer games. The close kinship between law and gaming is an idea that's been stirring in my mind for quite some time now, so I hope you'll bear with me as I try to flesh it out.

For those who wisely avoided law school, let me quickly summarize what **precedent** is: A precedent is a legal ruling on a particular issue that can be used to help decide subsequent questions of law with similar issues. For instance, if a court is asked to decide whether a semiautomatic pistol is a legitimate weapon of self-defense, a previous ruling that revolvers were legitimate weapons of self-defense would be precedent. If the precedent is followed, it is called "binding." If the precedent is ignored, the new case is said to be "distinguished" from the old by certain new facts. For instance, the court might distinguish pistols from revolvers by pointing out that their ammunition capacity is much greater.

What does this have to do with role-playing games? Back in Chapter 1, I noted that the foundational role of the gamemaster was that of Judge, responsible for "ruling on grey areas not covered by the rules." The process of ruling on grey areas creates precedent - or what we call "house rules".

Is Your Game Common, or Civil?

How much precedent is going to matter will depend on whether your game is a "common law" or "civil law" game.

"Common law" originated in Old England as a history of legal rules created by judges when deciding disputes. The judges began with the traditional customs of how matters had been handled, and then over time built up a body of law based on those past precedents. Common law generally has little or no basis in anything written, except perhaps a foundational Constitution or some scattered medieval statutes. The main disadvantage of a common law system is that there is no written "code" that citizens can consult to understand the laws of the land.

On the other hand, "civil law" originated in the Roman Empire as a collection or code of statutes created by legislatures. Judges interpret the statutes, but their rulings are not said to create law. The main disadvantage of a civil law system is that citizens can't depend on different judges to interpret the law the same way each time there's a case.

Faced with a question, a purely common-law court will look up what the court said last time it was confronted by a similar question. Meanwhile, a purely civil law court will look up what the most relevant statute says about the question and interpret it as it thinks best. Since each system has weaknesses, most legal systems today use a mix of both civil and common law, with legislators creating the overall framework of statutes, while judges fill in the gaps using common law methods based on precedent. Under this system, citizens can look at statutes to learn the baseline of the law, and then refer to past cases to understand how judges have previously ruled.

The analogy to a gamemaster in a tabletop game should, I hope, be clear. The game designer is the legislator; the game rules are the civil law; the citizens are the players; and the decisions of the gamemaster about grey areas in the rules are the common law. A gamemaster running a rules-light game like *Savage Worlds* or *Basic Fantasy* will end up acting mostly like a common law judge, forced to make rulings about particular situations without written statutes. In this case, precedent matters a lot. Fairness demands precedent.

FAIRNESS DEMANDS PRECEDENT

To prove this point, let's illustrate what happens when precedent is ignored. Imagine that you are running *Basic Fantasy*, a rules light game modeled after the classic 1980s editions of *Basic Dungeons & Dragons*. During a desperate retreat, Marcus, the party's fighter, wants to jump across a 15' chasm to safety. "Fighters jumping across chasms" is not covered by the rules. You decide that this is a test of heroic agility best resolved with an ability check against Dexterity. If Marcus rolls less than his Dexterity he will succeed; if not he will fail and plummet to his death. Marcus rolls a 9, less than his Dexterity of 12, and succeeds.

Next round, Quintus, the magic-user, decides he too wants to escape across the chasm. You again consult your rulebook and note that "magic-users jumping across chasms" is not covered by the rules. You decide that this is clearly a test of herculean strength, and demand an ability check against Strength. Quintus, with a Strength of 7, fails the roll, and his player demands to know why Marcus got to roll against Dexterity but he had to roll against Strength for the same task.

What can you say to this criticism? That you're the GM, your word is law, and it's your right to rule however you like on situations not covered by the rules? That there is no written rule stating which attribute is to be used in resolving the success of jumps, so this is completely fair? You can certainly **say** that, but it's unlikely to persuade the player of poor dead Quintus.

Let's now imagine that a couple weeks have passed, and the party must now, once again, jump across this chasm. You once again check the rules and again see no game mechanic specifying the chances of success. You announce that each character has a 2 in 6 chance of falling in, but otherwise they jump across successfully. Morne, who has both 18 Dexterity and Strength, demands to know why he now has a 33% chance of falling in, and not the 10% chance he'd have if you stuck with either of your two past rulings. You shrug. "There's no rule that says it has to be an ability check," you say.

It should be obvious that this is not a healthy manner in which to run a game. A game run like this is a game that lacks fairness, common sense, and verisimilitude. Yet it's very common when playing a rules-light game to experience this sort of arbitrary decision-making on the part of the gamemaster out of an insistence that "there aren't really any rules!" This attitude derives from a failure to recognize that, just like a common law judge creates law when he decides a case, **a gamemaster creates rules when he makes rulings**. Fairness to the players demands that the rules for any given situation be the same for each player in that situation.

RULES-LIGHT GAMES ARE JUST GAMES THAT HAVEN'T BEEN PLAYED A LOT YET

It's common to call games like *Basic Fantasy*, which heavily depend on the GM's judgment calls, rules-light games, in contrast to rules-heavy games like *Pathfinder*, which provide exhaustive mechanics. But with our deeper understanding of common law and civil law, we can see that a gamemaster's ruling is functionally a law, just like a game designer's rule is a law. Every rules-light game will over time become heavier with rules as its judge makes decisions about how things work. Rules-light and rules-heavy are only descriptive of the starting state of the game.

This being the case, when you are running a long-term campaign, you should remember that every time you issue a ruling, you have added to the "common law" of the game design. You should write down your rulings, and apply them again to similar situations in the future - or distinguish them from prior rulings to explain why they aren't being applied. The very best gamemasters do this so consistently that over time their long-running campaigns begin to develop an entire body of house rules covering the many special situations that have arisen in their campaign. Sometimes an entirely new RPG develops.

Indeed, my own body of *D&D* jurisprudence, developed over hundreds of sessions of *Classic D&D*, ultimately became the *Adventurer Conqueror King System*. Of course, my efforts with *ACKS* are nothing compared to the old masters. After all, the entire corpus of *Advanced Dungeons & Dragons* is just Gary Gygax and crew's common law rulings on *Original Dungeons & Dragons*. Even more impressive, the legendary skill-based RPG *Runequest* began as a set of house-rules for *D&D!* The transitional *D&D*-to-*Runequest* house rules were called the Perrin Conventions, named for *Runequest*'s lead designer Steve Perrin, and you can still find them on the web.

So next time you look at that sleek little rules-light game you just bought and think about what a breeze it's going to be to play, remember that it's not really rules-light. You just haven't played it enough yet to make it rules-heavy.

CHAPTER 14

RULES LAWYERING

In Chapter 13, we discussed the role of legal precedent in sustaining a long-running campaign, and explored how as a gamemaster, when you make rulings on grey areas not covered by the rules, you are acting just like a common law judge does in the US and UK court systems. In other words, the gamemaster is the game's judge in a literal, not figurative, sense. With that base established, I now want to expand our discussion of judging a game to address the phenomenon known as "rules lawyering."

Rules lawyering is the practice of using technicalities or ambiguities within the game rules to gain an advantage within the game; those who practice it are known as "rules lawyers." Rules lawyers crop up in every game. If playing a rules-light game, the rules lawyer will take advantage of ambiguities and vagueness inherent in whatever simple system is being used. If playing a rules-heavy game, the rules lawyer will take advantage of technicalities that are often overlooked in the volumes of text, or of ambiguities regarding how different rules interact. Either way, rules lawyers are so common that they are one of the basic player types covered in pretty much every guide to gamers there is.

Many gamemasters, who dislike the "litigation" involved in handling a rules lawyer, treat the rules lawyer as an enemy to be crushed or banned from the game; but rules lawyers don't need to be the enemy of good gaming. Indeed, a good rules lawyer can make the campaign better.

Most rules lawyers are not trying to gain an advantage within the game out of malice or spite; they are doing it because they are invested in the game and want to express their interest in the outcomes of the rules system. And that's a good thing! To put it bluntly, if a player's character is at stake, and he doesn't try to find some technicality to save his life, that player probably doesn't give a whit for your campaign.

There are, of course, problem players who use rules lawyering as their tool to cause grief. But there are also problem players who use role-playing to cause grief ("that's what my character would do"), ignorance to cause grief ("I didn't know that pulling the lever would get you killed") and so on. The issue is always the griefing, not the way the griefing is expressed. I've already discussed how to handle griefers in Chapter 10, and here we're focusing on non-griefing rules lawyers.

The classic example of good rules lawyering is when the players think of unexpected and unforeseen combinations of rules mechanics that create intriguing possibilities. Consider an example that came up in my own *Classic Dungeons & Dragons* campaign: What happens if a *levitating* wizard conjures a *floating disc*, and then has friend stand on the *floating disc* and push the wizard with a 10' pole? For some reason, the authors of *Classic D&D* did not think this activity merited a specific rule, leaving me to decide what the outcome of this adventure in arcane aeronautics would be.

As a gamemaster, you will be called on to make decisions like this every single session, and when your campaign is young, probably every single encounter. The rules lawyers in your group can be counted on to always advocate for their benefit, but you should not do likewise - it will not do to always side with the players, nor always against them. Instead, you must strive to interpret the rule in a consistent way (for all the reasons I pointed out last chapter). How does one do this?

THE CANONS OF STATUTORY INTERPRETATION

Well, for starters, put away your Freud and Derrida. While it has long been intellectually hip to put on a black beret, drink French martinis, and declare that "text has no meaning," this sort of deconstruction is of little use to an RPG gamemaster charged with interpreting what the game rules say.

A better source of guidance are the "canons of statutory interpretation" used by real-world judges as rules of thumb to determine the meaning of laws. A thorough discussion of the canons takes about fifty pages, but below, I offer some simplified canons of statutory interpretation that can be used by a gamemaster to interpret game rules:

1. Your starting point in interpreting rules is always the plain language employed by the game designer.

2. If a rule specifically defines a term, use the defined definition; but in the absence of a defined definition, interpret the rule in accordance with the ordinary and natural meaning of the language (the dictionary definition).

3. If the rule is still ambiguous, look at the rule holistically. Terminology in a rule that is ambiguous in isolation may be clarified if the same terminology is used elsewhere in a context that makes its meaning clear, or because only one of the possible meanings is compatible with the rest of the game.

4. Gamemasters should not interpret different terms within the same rule to mean the same thing, nor the same term within the same rule to mean different things.

5. If the literal interpretation of the words is absurd, the rule must be interpreted to avoid absurdity.

6. If possible, give meaning to every clause and word of a rule; don't assume anything is redundant.

7. Specific rules override general rules.

Let's apply these canons to the case of the *levitating* wizard and his friend pushing him from a nearby *floating disc*. The wizard, a consummate rules lawyer, argued that he would move horizontally through the air from the push, while his *disc* (carrying his friend) would follow, enabling them to create a two-man "fly cycle" that could maneuver through the air.

We start with the plain language of the rules, as it appeared in the version of *Classic D&D* we were playing at the time:

> *Floating Disc*: This spell creates an invisible magical platform the size and shape of a small round shield which can carry up to 500 pounds of weight. The disc will be created at the height of the caster's waist, and will remain at that height, following the caster wherever he goes. If the caster goes further than 6 feet from the disc, it will automatically follow, with a movement rate equal to the caster's.

> *Levitate*: When this spell is cast, the caster may move up or down in the air without any support. Motion up or down is at a rate of 20' per round. This spell does not enable the caster to move from side-to-side. The caster could, however, levitate to a ceiling and move sideways by using his hands.

In the situation at hand, the caster is *levitating* in the air, while his friend is standing on the *disc* about 6' away pushing him with a 10' stick. Since a *disc* is the size and shape of a shield and can carry 500 pounds, the plain language of the rule (Canon #1) makes it clear that the friend can stand on the disc. The first real question is what happens to the caster when his friend pushes him?

Levitation plainly says that the spell does "not enable" the caster to move from side-to-side. "Not enable" is not a defined term so, following Canon #2, we look to the dictionary definition. "Not enable" in this sentence could mean "not permit" or "not empower". If it means "not permit," then levitation forbids side to side movement. But if it means "not empower" then *levitation* simply doesn't provide the motive force for side to side movement, but it doesn't forbid it. Since the very next sentence says the caster could "move sideways by using his hands", looking at the rule holistically (as per Canon #3) tells us that "not enable" simply means "not empower" because that's the only way that permitting moving hand by hand across the ceiling would make sense.

Canon #4 tells us that we should not interpret the same term to mean different things, so there's nothing preventing the caster from moving sideways while *levitating* if some other motive force is provided. We rule that if crawling across the ceiling will move a *levitating* caster, so will getting pushed by a big stick.

The second question is what will happen to the friend on the *floating disc*. The plain language says that "if the caster goes further than 6 feet from the disc, it will automatically follow, with a movement rate equal to the caster's." The plain language thus suggests that when the caster is shoved away by the pole, the disc will follow at the caster's movement rate. But what is the caster's movement rate? Here things get quite tricky!

"Movement rate" is a defined term in the *D&D Basic Rules*, so following Canon #2 we look at the defined definition: "The number of feet a character may move in one turn." The normal movement rate is that "all characters are able to move 120' in one turn." Our rules lawyer argues that this means that the wizard and his friend can move 120' per turn by pushing the caster. But this makes no sense - pushing hard enough to send the wizard gliding 120' would surely do damage to him, or knock the fighter off the disc, or both; or that interpretation would also make it possible for the disc to move further than the caster. Since the literal interpretation of the words is absurd, we follow Canon #5, and interpret the rule to avoid absurdity. We rule that "movement rate" means the distance the caster actually moved, not his possible movement rate. In this case, that's about 4-5' since he's being pushed from 6' away with a 10' pole.

The final question is what will happen if the caster levitates up or down? Reverting to Canon #1, the plain text says "the disc will be created at the height of the caster's waist, and will remain at that height, following the caster wherever he goes. If the caster goes further than 6 feet from the disc, it will automatically follow." Since vertical movement could take the caster further than 6 feet from the disc, and since the disc "will remain" at the height of the caster's waist, the disc will move up or down with the caster.

Following this chain of interpretation, we can rule in a consistent way that the wizard and his friend can move 20' up or down each round, and about 5' horizontally each round, creating a slow-moving "fly cycle" that lets the two of them avoid pits and soar over obstacles.

This ruling ultimately led to my campaign featuring a *flying* centaur under *invisibility 10' radius* carrying 2 wizards each with 4 *floating discs* carrying archers, resulting in a D&D stealth bomber...But that is another story.

CHAPTER 15
VIOLENCE & VISCERA

Just before I wrote this chapter, I had the chance to take a weekend off to attend MACE, a local RPG convention at Highpoint, North Carolina. While in my day-to-day gaming I am generally a gamemaster, at MACE I made an effort to play under as many different GMs using as many different systems as possible - everything from unreleased story games to *D6 Adventure* to *Savage Worlds* to *Pathfinder*. Playing in an RPG when you're usually a GM is something like watching a play when you normally work stage crew - part of the time you're immersed in the experience, but part of the time you're watching to see how the tricks are being pulled off.

One of the things I perennially notice when I play is the high variability around whether combat is **fun** or not. At MACE, I played in one session that used a combat-oriented rules set, and yet the combat was dull and uninteresting; while in another session, a game with the simplest of combat rules had exciting and fun fight scenes. Why might that be? As part of our discussion of the art of game mastering, let's find out.

WHAT'S IN IT FOR ME?

Combat encounters are, as a general rule, the most complex and time-consuming rules element of any RPG. (Certain extended scenes of role-playing may, of course, take longer than a fight, but this is not usually due to the rules.) When running lengthy and complex activities, unfortunately, it's easy to lose your players' attention. Concentration is hard, and the lure of munchies, doodling, or - even worse - mobile phones is strong. Every player is continuously tuned into the radio station WINI FM, or "What's in it for me?" Players will pay sharp attention to facts and details that relate to their character, but they quickly tune out if they deem the information or action irrelevant to them. As a result, it's all too often the case that during a combat encounter, only the currently active player and the gamemaster are paying attention at any given moment, while the rest of the players are sitting there bored, merely waiting for their turn to have fun. Worse, they might be actively disrupting the game with side chat!

So, how can this be overcome? While there are many techniques that are specific to individual games, there are a few techniques that work in every game. They are high stakes and vivid imagery - the violence and the viscera of a combat encounter.

THE STAKES MUST BE REAL!

As I discussed at length in Chapter 2, RPGs must offer their participants real choices with meaningful consequences, not merely the illusion of challenge. This is doubly important in combat! And yet most game masters practicing today will openly admit that they pre-balance the encounters, fudge the dice, and change the rules to ensure the players win. Then they wonder why their players are bored...

When I run combat, the stakes are always real. Beloved henchmen are brutally slain. Favored magic items are destroyed, never to be seen again. Heroic sacrifices can be in vain, and the entire party can be wiped out no matter how invested the players may be (in my Auran Empire campaign, nearly everyone was slain in a penultimate fight against the arch-villain in the 67th session, leaving the survivors thirsty for climactic revenge.) If you want your combat to be exciting, leave the outcome of the fight uncertain and make sure the stakes really matter.

In offering this advice, I fully acknowledge that I am both a reactionary and a contrarian. Since the beginning of the Hickman Revolution in 1984, most RPGs have gravitated towards removing actual risk from the game in the interest of allowing the players to experience an ongoing narrative with some certainty that they will see its finish. Loss and death are considered "not fun" and excluded from the gaming experience. The trend towards reducing the risk of permanent loss accelerated thereafter. By the time D&D reached its Fourth Edition, not only was it nearly impossible for a player character to die, but rust monsters didn't even permanently destroy items any more because it was "not fun" to lose gear.

I believe that this, more than any other trend, explains why RPG combat is so often boring. If the players will always win, then why should they bother to pay attention or even care? Answer: They shouldn't and won't.

To be clear, I am not saying that every combat must put the entire party at risk of being slain. Making every encounter into a pitched battle with existential stakes is just as destructive to player agency as making every battle a victory: Players need to be able to make choices that can lead to easy wins, too.

No, what I am saying is that every combat should put the entire party at the risk of losing whatever should be at risk of loss in the game world. There are four broad levels of risk:

1. Strategic Position
2. Assets
3. Character
4. Party

When an encounter risks "strategic position," it means that the circumstances under which the player characters are adventuring may change for the worse if the encounter is not handled smartly. For instance, if your mid-level adventurers encounter goblin scouts with war-horns, they will almost certainly win the encounter, but they risk winning it only after the scouts have sounded the alarm.

When an encounter risks "assets," it means that survival of every player character is likely but the participants might lose things they value. This could be treasure, vehicles, pets, henchmen, magic items, and so on. An encounter with a rust monster in *Classic Dungeons & Dragons* is an asset risk encounter. If your players choose to take on a rust monster, the consequences of item loss need to be real.

When an encounter risks "characters," it means that survival of the party as a whole is likely, but individual player characters might die or be irreparably harmed. An encounter with energy-draining undead in *Classic Dungeons & Dragons* could be a character risk encounter, as even a victorious party might experience real harm.

When an encounter risks "party," it means that the survival of the party as a whole is in question. Losing this fight will mean that every character is killed and the campaign is over.

If you've been "trusting in the Fudge," i.e. fudging your dice and outcomes, try putting something at stake in your next battle. It doesn't take much to get the players to sit up straight and get involved in the combat. The moment they realize they could lose *something*, they start to pay attention. And if they realize they could lose *everything*, the increase in intensity is palpable.

As a rule of thumb, you can tell whether you've run a great fight by how the players react to someone getting the killing blow on a monster. If they're bitter that they weren't the "cool kid" who got the kill, then there was no real risk - they were just competing narcissistically amongst themselves. If they are fist-bumping the player who got the killing blow and cheering with relief, then you ran a great fight.

THE SPECTACLE MUST BE AWESOME!

RPGs are always described as games of the imagination, in which the players and the gamemaster weave the action and imagery with their words. And yet, all too often, combat is just run by the numbers: "Bob, roll to hit." "14! I hit it. I did 8 damage." "OK, the orc dies. Jim, you're up next." Such a fight can be intellectually stimulating, if you're a wargamer, and it can be worth paying attention to, if the stakes are real, but it is nevertheless lacking in emotional punch.

Given that everyone comes into RPGs wanting to use their imagination, the reasons why combat devolves to simple mechanics are somewhat mysterious to me. I think it may be because nothing is at stake. It's hard to conjure up the energy for vivid imagery when it doesn't really matter. Whatever the reason, running a role-playing game by the numbers is a crime akin to serving chips without salsa: Violators should be taken out and shot. Violence demands viscera!

Now, I am fortunate in that I have, through long practice, refined the art for conjuring up visceral violence nearly at will. "You swing your iron-flanged mace into the orc's chin, the force of the blow smashing so hard that its teeth shatter into sharp shards that embed themselves in its bloody cheeks. Then the orc's axe carves your belly open, and your intestines leak out like wet, pulpy worms." See, it just flows out. For the less practiced, I've prepared a short list of rules of thumb to help you out.

Brutal Blows: Most games will feature results that represent especially brutal blows - a critical hit, max damage, death blows, and so on. **If you narrate nothing else, narrate these.** Aim for body horror - the graphic destruction of the body. I've found the most visceral reactions come from gruesome penetration of soft, pulpy body parts, or the shattering of bones that we all secretly fear breaking. Go for thrusts through the soft palate of the upper mouth or the loose skin of the neck; impacts on the fragile bones of the knee-cap or elbow; slashes through the tender skin of the belly. Carve off the breasts and leave them dangling, crack open the cranium and have grey jelly spray outward, shatter the spine and let spinal fluid leak onto the floor.

Hits: Every good hit deserves a good description. However, many RPGs, most especially those based on *D&D*, give creatures the ability to survive dozens of hits. If every successful attack is narrated as a brutal blow, the result can become silly, as no one could still be standing after that much trauma. When narrating a hit that's not a critical or a kill, focus on damage to the target's armor and shield, its state of pain or fatigue, and its position. "With a metallic crunch, your mace slams into his shield, leaving a dent. The knight swears in pain and recoils backward." Fortunately, the English language leaves us no shortage for words you can use to describe the backward movement after an attack: Fall back, lurch, stagger, recoil, withdraw, retreat, and limp are all words to remember. So are descriptions of equipment damage such as blunt, break, dent, bang, splinter, crack, and tear.

Misses: Nothing is so frustrating for the player as to miss an attack that he has waited all round to roll for. Even worse is when his narration is "ok, you miss. Steve, you're up." You owe it to the player to explain why his adventurer missed. If he's a highly experienced fighter, it's because the opponent fell back, or put up a desperate defense: "Still reeling from your last slash, the orc retreats before your onslaught. You can't penetrate his defenses but you both know his time is coming soon." If it's because he's a novice, your narration will reflect that: "Your blood is pumping with the heat of combat, and you over-extend your sword blow."

Near Misses: If you roll a near miss on the player, a great rule of thumb is to vividly describe the attack before you provide the mechanical outcome. If the player knows you missed him, there's no tension no matter how vivid your imagery. But if he's not sure yet whether you missed, he will hang onto every word for a clue as to what's coming.

Player Character Death: If you're following my recommendations for play with real consequences, player character death can and will happen. Here's what not to do: **Don't** focus on the numbers, **don't** express contrition, and **don't** move quickly on to the next event. A player character deserves a death worthy of the sagas, a memorable death that will be talked about forever. Now is the time to pull out all the stops! Combine all of the recommendations in brutal blows above with foreshadowing of darkness, vengeance, and rage. If a troll rends the character to death, then what happens is that "you scream in agony as the troll's claws dig deep into your shoulders, deeper until finally it tears outward and your torso is rended into three parts, left and right arms spinning outward as a torrent of blood and lymph flows from your shattered rib cage. In a final act of defiance, you spit once more into the troll's face, then fall into to blackness."

Slow Motion: One of the coolest techniques you can achieve through vivid narration is the effect of *300*-style fighting, with its alternating sequences of slow motion and high speed violence. The trick here is to use the present continuous verb tense ("is cutting") when describing slow motion sequences, and the present tense ("cuts") for fast action. "Marcus is leaping through the air, his blade is cutting to the left and right, gutting an orc with each slash, and then suddenly he lands and thrusts forward and his sword impales the orc chieftain through the heart."

If these ideas don't directly help you, turn to your favorite books and movies and take notes on how the authors and directors show fight scenes. Take your notes into your next session, and make things visceral! With practice, you will develop your own repertoire of techniques to make your RPG battles come alive. It's worth the effort. **If there's one place that the art of storytelling can make more difference than any other, it's in RPG combat.**

CHAPTER 16
FACTORING IN THE FUDGE

Every time a gamemaster picks up the dice, he is toying with fate - the fate of the players, the fate of the adversaries, the fate of the campaign world. When the dice come up in ways that are unexpected or create situations that are uncomfortable or unwanted, the temptation hangs omnipresent to say the dice said something they did not - to fudge.

Back in Chapter 1, I explained why you should never fudge a meaningful die roll, noting "the desire to fudge is founded on the faulty premise that you need to make sure people have fun. But it's a mistake to believe that letting a character die destroys fun... It's fudging the dice that destroys fun, by destroying the ability for the players to make meaningful choices."

In this chapter, I want to discuss when you should fudge. Obviously, if you should never fudge a meaningful die roll, the universe of available fudging is limited to **meaningless** die rolls. But many die rolls are meaningless, or seemingly meaningless. Should you fudge some of them? All of them?

The short answer is that you can fudge a die roll when it benefits play without impacting the ability of the players to make meaningful choices. As an illustration of this general point, here are three situations where fudging makes sense.

#1: Fudging for Speed When the Outcome Is Virtually Certain

Sometimes, the outcome of a situation is virtually certain. For instance, imagine that there are eight player characters about to attack one easy-to-hit adversary with only 2 hit points remaining. The first player character, Marcus, hits and inflicts 1 point of damage. In this circumstance, it might be appropriate for the GM to "fudge" the adversary's remaining hp so that Marcus's damage is enough to kill, in the interest of speed of play. After all, the adversary is going to die regardless, and depending on the system, going through the attack routine of another character will just waste a lot of time that might be better spent on more meaningful play.

Note that I said it *might* be appropriate to fudge. But it might not be. If the adversary is a notorious warlord, and whoever lands the killing blow will earn much honor, then who lands the killing blow is meaningful. Or if Marcus wanted to kill the adversary, but his comrade Quintus, acting next in the round, wanted to capture him, then the fact that Marcus didn't kill the adversary is very meaningful indeed.

A quick way to determine whether fudging for speed is appropriate is to ask, "If I just narrated this outcome without a die roll, would any player be deprived of meaningful choice and would any player character experience a meaningful difference in the game world?" If the answer is no, fudge away.

#2 Fudging for Verisimilitude when the Alternative is Inconsistency

Campaign worlds can range from the gonzo (in which internal consistency matters less than the "wow factor", so that you might have space aliens riding psychic dinosaurs) to the naturalistic (in which internal consistency trumps the wow factor). But even at their most gonzo, most campaign worlds aim for some sense of verisimilitude, that is, some quality of realism, and the need for realism is reflected in much of the "mechanics" of game play.

The wandering monster tables for the *Classic Dungeons & Dragons* rules, for instance, make it more likely to encounter crocodiles near rivers and mountain lions near mountains; and more likely to encounter ordinary animals than to encounter ancient red dragons overall. Thus even a naturalistic GM can use these wandering monster tables and have assurance that the will produce results that have some sense of verisimilitude or internal consistency. But sometimes even the best mechanics produce results that make no sense.

For instance, imagine that at the start of a wilderness adventure, only a few miles from the adventure's starting village, the very first random encounter is the lair of an ancient red dragon (a 1 in a 1000 event that comes to pass.) This poses a tremendous challenge to the GM: Why is there an ancient red dragon just a few miles from the starting village, and why did no one know about it? Now, the GM might decide to run with this result. He might decide the dragon had only recently moved in, and its presence was not yet known; or that its presence had always been known, but that talking about it was a taboo, so the villagers hadn't warned the PCs; or that the villagers were actually evil cultists in cahoots with the dragon, and the adventurers were just another sacrifice sent to die. All of these are examples of excellence in improvisational play.

But it's also possible that the GM had previously established to the players that this was a safe village, with a sage who had briefed the party on local lore; and that the party's clerics had already used magic to ascertain the villager's good intentions. In this case, the dice have created a situation that makes no sense within the context of what's gone before. Here, the GM could fudge the dice to create a realistic situation.

Now, it might be suggested that this fudging has deprived the players of meaningful choice - for instance, of the chance to interact with the red dragon. But as I noted at length in Chapter 12, **fairness demands precedent**. The players in your game cannot make meaningful choices if the world can shift around them with no apparent consistency. There are times when consistency must trump randomness.

#3 Fudging to Fix What You've Screwed Up

As a gamemaster, you will screw up. It happens to the best of us. At some point the caffeine-induced high will wear off, the Doritos will mess with your synaptic speed, and you'll accidentally forget that a Gargantuan Kraken gets to do both standard damage and bonus constriction damage when grappling with a tentacle. Because of this mistake, the situation in the game world will bear no relation to what it would have been had you not erred. If you value consistency and realism in your game play (or are simply a compulsive perfectionist), this is a traumatic moment.

In the face of this situation, you can simply ignore the error and keep playing. This is fine in most cases, but if your error has been egregious and involves critical aspects of the game (or major adversaries), it won't be acceptable. Your second option is to "rewind" gameplay - but this is often impossible. Your third option is to fudge some die rolls to get things back on track.

For example, if you realize you've been rolling only half the appropriate amount of damage for the villain, you might fudge some damage rolls to be higher over the next few rounds. Or, if you accidentally have been hitting a player character you actually missed, you could fudge your next few attack rolls to insure some misses occur.

It's important to keep in mind the goal of this sort of fudging: You are not trying to alter the outcome to fit some preconceived notion of what the dice ought to have rolled. You are, rather, adjusting the dice to fix errors you created. Done properly, the outcome should be close to what would have happened if you'd never erred at all.

#4 Fudging at the Final Frontier

I'm not sure there are any other circumstances where fudging makes sense in the context of agency-driven sandbox play. There might be, but I haven't encountered them if so. The three above are by far the most common ones I encounter. But every campaign is a law unto itself, and you might face situations I haven't thought of that demand fudging. Be cautious but do what you deem best to maintain player agency and your world in motion.

CHAPTER 17
THE SECRET ART OF ABDUCTION

This chapter is about the secret of abduction. No, not alien abduction. And not kidnapping people, either. I mean abduction as in abductive reasoning. Abduction is defined by Wikipedia as "the process of arriving at an explanatory hypothesis of a surprising circumstance." The foremost philosopher of abduction, Charles Sanders Peirce, summarized abduction as follows:

> The surprising fact, C, is observed;
> But if A were true, C would be a matter of course;
> Hence, there is reason to suspect that A is true.

For instance, assume the surprising circumstance that my car won't start this morning. If it were true that my car battery were dead, then the fact that my car won't start would be a matter of course. So there is reason to suspect (abduce) that my car battery is dead.

At its core, abduction is guesswork, but it forms the basis of all natural science, medical diagnosis, and indeed much of human thought. When Newton developed the laws of gravity based on observing the motion of falling bodies, he was using abductive reasoning. When a physician is presented with a set of symptoms and diagnoses an illness to explain the symptoms, he is using abductive reasoning.

Abduction is also the method used by conspiracy theorists worldwide when they observe surprising facts about our world and piece together sinister explanations for them. America has its share of conspiracy theorists, such as 9/11 Truthers, but it is in Italy that conspiracy theory has been refined to its finest art form. The Italians have coined the word *dietrologia* for the art of finding hidden motives to explain seemingly everyday events. As explained in the Guardian, "rampant suspicion is the reason Italians love the dinner party game of dietrologia, in which participants try to out-trump each other with paranoid ideas..."

We have much to learn from the dietrologists, for abduction is the secret art of the greatest gamemasters. Abduction is what transforms random tables and wandering monsters into a living, breathing game world. Abduction is what transforms a hodge-podge of materials into a coherent campaign. It is the art of finding explanations that make the campaign better. You must study this art, and master it, the way Miyamato Musashi studied sword-fighting.

FINDING EXPLANATIONS THAT MAKE THE CAMPAIGN BETTER

In Chapter 9, I discussed the oracular power of dice, and noted that the key to using random events in your game is to interpret the random event in the context of what's come before it. Any time you do that, you are practicing abduction. But abduction can explain your own choices, too.

For example, in my Auran Empire campaign, my party of adventurers began exploring another world in their crystal sphere, inhabited with strange and alien beings. To fill up this new world, I began liberally adapting unused encounters and dungeons from other products and places. One such encounter, from a hastily-chosen free adventure I had downloaded, involved an ettin in a jail cell. Ettins are common enough in the Auran

Empire from whence the adventurers hailed, but were not a creature that was native to the alien world they were now on.

Now, outside of the context of the game, the reason an ettin appeared is simply that I accidentally put him somewhere he shouldn't have been. The encounter he was a part of had been created for a different dungeon in a different campaign, where his presence would not have been surprising. But on the alien world, his presence was odd indeed and demanded justification or removal. I could have simply changed the ettin into another creature more appropriate to the new world. But I didn't - instead, I abduced why an ettin might be present.

So, the surprising fact: An ettin on an alien world.

My abduction: If there were a mysterious gate through spacetime that swept up creatures from the Auran Empire and deposited them on the alien world, the presence of an ettin would be a matter of course.

My conclusion: There is reason to suspect that a mysterious gate through spacetime exists on the alien world.

By simply importing a legacy encounter from an old dungeon I had lying around, I had suddenly concluded that a mysterious portal existed somewhere that brings in creatures from the old world to the new. If I had simply changed the ettin into an alien, this portal would not have existed, and the game world would have been a less interesting place.

Note that I did not start with the idea of the portal - I started with the arbitrary appearance of the creature. This is not cause-effect reasoning; it's the opposite. It's finding an explanation for something that didn't have one - an explanation that makes the campaign (hopefully) better.

MAKING ABDUCTION WORK FOR YOU

The art of abduction depends on having a set of "surprising facts," that is, a circumstance you need to explain. Fortunately, such facts are never in short supply. Indeed, the easiest and most accessible method of brainstorming available to any gamemaster is random generation of facts. Hundreds of game accessories, in print or online, can randomly generate content for you - random adventure generators, random magic swords, random taverns, random jewelry, random monsters, and on and on.

For example, with a single click on the random adventure generator above, I created a dungeon called "The Weird Citadel of Secrets" with many rooms. One of these was Room 45, which noted "there are cracks in the floor here" and "treasure: 500sp, 20gp." The surprising fact here is "there is treasure in an otherwise empty room with cracks in the floor." I abduced that "if the treasure belonged to adventurers who had fallen into the cracks in the floor, this would make sense." And, presto! The cracks in the floor became large, menacing cracks which must have broken under the feet of some hapless hero, whose precious wealth lingers there still. This is the oracular power of the dice at work!

Another great source of "surprising facts" is through adaptation - porting content from other sources into your campaign setting. For instance, in the Auran Empire, I've made use of old *D&D* modules such as *Isle of Dread, Against the Giants,* and *City of the Gods,* each of which came from a different campaign setting (Mystara, Greyhawk, and Blackmoor respectively). You can do the same with articles from *Dragon* and *Dungeon* magazines or various internet sources; modules from other game systems; ideas stolen from your favorite TV shows, movies, and books; or anything else you can take inspiration from! My ettin from earlier is a great example of this.

A third method of generating "surprising facts" is to rely on your players, who are endlessly dietrological. In one session of *Cyberpunk 2020,* the player characters were on a cargo transport mission when they were attacked by three commandos carrying smartguns. One player wondered aloud, "How did these guys find us?" Another player figured it out: "There must be tracking emitters in the cargo we're carrying!" The group immediately scanned its precious cargo, and learned that, indeed, there were tracking emitters hidden in the cargo that had led their enemies to their location.

Except, of course, there were no tracking emitters until that moment; before then, there was no "it" to figure out at all. The commandos were merely a random encounter (random encounter 00 on the After Midnight Encounters in Night City table, to be exact). I hadn't yet abduced why or how the commandos were tracking the player characters when the encounter began; all I knew when I ran the encounter was that the random table said there was a commando attack. I rewarded what I saw as an insightful act of abduction by the players. Because they had been "correct" that there were tracking emitters, the player characters were able to remove them.

ABDUCTION ON THE GO

Abductive reasoning is so powerful and useful that you can use it to run entire adventures on the fly. All you need is a bunch of interesting and completely unconnected events and a bit of imagination. Indeed, the session of *Cyberpunk 2020* I described above was made up on the fly when I grabbed a copy of the *Night City Sourcebook* and rolled some random encounters. I rolled that "a convoy of US Army troops rolls up from South of Night City... towards an embarkation point" and "an agent on the corner is recruiting parties of cyberpunks to move small, valuable commodities from Night City to various parts of the world." From there I abduced that the agent had ties to the US Army and was selling a "surplus" of the very same commodities that the US Army troops were carrying.

That abduction instantly lead to other considerations - were there military police that were aware of the agents' activities who will seek to re-capture the "surplus?" Were the buyers enemies of the US who couldn't be trusted to leave the cyberpunks alive after the transaction? Were the "surplus" goods of such value as military hardware that the players might want to steal the whole shipment?

It was with these considerations in mind that I abduced that the random encounter with commandos was related to the cargo that the cyberpunks were carrying. In a different context, a different abduction would have been merited.

Abduction, then, is truly a black art - akin to the quantum mechanics of a role-playing game world. Explanations for the facts of the game world may not exist until they are consciously observed; until then they are merely potential explanations, ideas floating in the seas of possibility. Abduction is how you plunge into the ocean of ideas and find the best ones to explain the facts you're dealing with in your game.

At this point, you might have realized that I've shown you how to get some facts with which to generate abductive conclusions; and I've given you examples of my own abductive reasoning; and I've given you some suggestions of how to use it to run spontaneous games; but I haven't actually explained how to abduce. But that, sadly, I cannot explain: It's an intuitive leap. As Musashi said in *The Book of Five Rings*, "it cannot be clearly explained in writing. You must practice diligently in order to understand."

CHAPTER 18

SMASHING THE SYSTEM

A "smash-up," also known as a mash-up, bootleg, blend, cut-up, crossover, or powermix, is a song or composition created when a producer blends a pair (or more) of previously existing songs, generally by combining the vocal track from one song with the instrumental track of another. Smash-ups have been around a long time but became a 21st century cultural phenomenon with 2004's Grey Album, a smash-up by Danger Mouse of Jay-Z's Black Album and the Beatles' White Album. Nowadays they are practically high art.

Smash-ups are not confined to music, of course. Videogames have smash-ups (often called "mods") and so do tabletop RPGs. Smashing up RPGs has been defined as "replacing major rules components with components from different games" or "taking two games in your collection and mixing them together." However you define it, it's a lot of fun; indeed, one of my favorite pastimes as a gamemaster is blending systems and settings to create something unique. It's a way to set your campaign apart from everything else out there, and I recommend every gamemaster delve into the art of the smash-up.

If you spend much time on gamer forums, you'll see some really humorous smash-ups. My personal favorite of all time is a smash-up of the esoteric fantasy games *Empire of the Petal Throne* and *Skyrealms of Jorune* to create *Skyrealms of Tekumel,* a "world so weird no one goes there at all."

Obviously, the writers are doing it just for giggles, but the key to any smash-up is to notice how two systems or settings fit together. I call this "finding the hook," and it's the first step in a three-part process:

1. Hook - You notice a rule mechanic or setting element from one game that somehow fits into the framework of the rules or setting of another game

2. Blend - You adapt the rule mechanic or setting element from the first game into the second game

3. Double Check - You review the adjacent rules or setting elements to make sure the smashed-up game is still coherent

It's easiest to explain in practice, so let's start smashing.

DRIVER: CAR WARS MEETS CLASSIC TRAVELLER

Let's begin with Steve Jackson's *Car Wars*, a widely played simulation of automobile combat in a post-apocalyptic future. While *Car Wars* is mostly about car combat, it features the skeletons of a role-playing system: Characters are rated with skills like "Gunner" and "Mechanic" with ratings from 0 to +5, while task resolution is resolved with a roll of 2d6 plus the skill level to meet a difficulty number. For instance, to hit with a machinegun requires a roll of 7 or greater, with the character's Gunner skill level added to the total of the dice.

As it happens, both this skill system and this task resolution are precisely mirrored in GDW's *Classic Traveller*, the influential science-fiction RPG. In *Classic Traveller*, characters are rated with skills like "Gunner" and "Mechanic" with ratings from 0 to +5, and task resolution is resolved with a roll of 2d6 plus the skill level to meet a difficulty number. This is our "hook" - we've noticed that the core mechanics of the two systems are identical.

What makes this interesting is that *Car Wars* offers virtually no character development around this system; on the other hand, *Classic Traveller* is famous for its character generation system, in which characters must go through a career path that can have them enter the military, gain promotions and commendations, earn rewards such as weapons, armor, or starships, and even die in the line of duty! (That's right - in *Classic Traveller*, your PC can die during character generation.) The obvious mash-up, then, would be to adapt the *Classic Traveller* career path system to *Car Wars*, replacing e.g. Space Marines with Autoduelists, Scouts with Outriders, and rewards like spaceships with automobiles. That's our "blend" - we're adapting the character generation from *Traveller* into *Car Wars*. We cleverly call this new system *Driver*.

Once the blend is written, the "double check" would be to assess what this would do to the adjacent rules. We note that *Classic Traveller* produces characters with on average 4 to 6 skills at +1, while *Car Wars* starts characters with 3 skills at +0. So our smash-up is going to create characters that are more competent than starting *Car Wars* characters. We make a note that to challenge characters created using our *Driver* system we'll need to make sure major NPCs are rolled up using a similar system.

As it happens, someone has actually done this smash-up; you can find it implemented at The Daemon Mechanic.

RUNEPUNK: CYBERPUNK MEETS RUNEQUEST

As our second smash-up, let's turn to Mike Pondsmith's *Cyberpunk 2020*. *Cyberpunk 2020* defined the cyberpunk genre in the late 1980s and early 1990s. One of its most widely-imitated mechanics is the concept of "cyberpsychosis" and "humanity loss." Each character in *Cyberpunk* has an Empathy attribute (abbreviated EMP), which controls persuasion, seduction, diplomacy, and other social skills (similar to D&D's Charisma score).

As characters are upgraded with cybernetics such as Boosted Reflexes or Grafted Muscles, they incur Humanity Loss, which permanently lowers their EMP. The more cybered up a character gets, the less able he is to interact with fellow humans. Characters whose EMP drops to 0 become "cyberpsychos" and are generally killed by elite *Blade Runner*-type cops. While EMP is not directly useful to combat or action-oriented characters, it serves as a cap on how upgraded such a character can become through cybernetics.

If you've played a lot of *Cyberpunk*, it's impossible to read the rules to Chaosium's *Runequest* without comparing that game's POW mechanic to *Cyberpunk*'s EMP. In *Runequest*, each character has a POW attribute (short for "Power") that measures their psychic strength. Characters need POW to cast spells, but they can also permanently sacrifice points of POW to bind demons, create magic items, and join cults. This is our "hook" - the similarity of EMP and POW. What if we had magical "cybernetics" that drained POW?

To "blend" them together, we sketch out the form of these "cybernetics." Inspired by the edgy aesthetic of *Cyberpunk*, we'll make them "flesh runes" (tattooed glyphs on the flesh) and "soul jewelry" (like magical rings and amulets, but they must be pierced through the flesh to have permanent effect). Like cybernetics, flesh runes and soul jewelry can augment a character's strength (Grafted Muscles) or speed (Boosted Reflexes), provide natural armor (Subdermal Armor), the ability to see in the dark (Nightvision Optics) and so on. Each of these upgrades will require a permanent sacrifice of POW, based on the benefit gained; if a character's POW drops to 0, he becomes a soulless zombie (the equivalent of a cyberpsycho).

Now we'll "double check." We note that a character's current POW is the basis for his magical resistance, meaning that characters which have "cybernetics" will be very susceptible to all forms of magic. Since this is very punitive and would make the flesh runes largely useless, we'll have to adjust the magic resistance rules - the easiest method probably being to have magic resistance be based on the character's POW plus the value of the POW imbued in any "cybernetics." Voila! *Runepunk.*

Like *Driver*, a version of *Runepunk* does exist - I ran it as a campaign in 2008! It was the very first game ever set in the Auran Empire setting. Interestingly enough, R. Talsorian Games has itself released a game which is nearly a perfect implementation of a Runepunk mash-up: *The Witcher RPG*, which combines the *Cyberpunk 2020* rules with the world of the *Witcher* novels.

SMASH THE SYSTEM!

Hopefully these two examples have demonstrated what smashing-up is all about. I'll end this chapter with some systems that I think are ripe for a smash-up:

- *Dragon Age RPG* and *GURPs*

- *Barbarians of Lemuria* and *Star Wars D6*

- *Marvel Super Heroes* and *Warhammer Fantasy Battle*

Once you know to start looking for smash-up hooks, your collection of RPGs transforms from "games you probably won't ever play" to "systems for the smashing". So start smashing!

CHAPTER 19
ARBITER OF WORLDS

In this closing chapter of the book, I want to review what we've discussed so far and then leave you with a call to action. Below I've taken the lessons of each chapter and summarized them to create one-paragraph canons of gamemastering.

THE CANONS OF GAMEMASTERING

1. The gamemaster has four roles: Judge, Worldbuilder, Adversary, and Storyteller. Of these, the most important function is that of judge. As judge, you are first and foremost responsible for explaining and enforcing the rules, preventing cheating, ruling on grey areas not covered by the rules, and controlling the flow of information about the world to the players.

2. It's not your job to make sure people have fun. It's your job to create an environment in which everyone could have fun. The best thing that a GM can do to make a fun environment is to allow their players to experience a sense of agency in the game world. Agency is the capacity for humans to make choices and impose those choices on the world. "Railroads" and "roller coasters" that offer an illusion of choice do not take advantage of the special virtue of tabletop RPGs to create agency. But agency requires more than just player freedom. It requires causality so that the player's free-willed choices are effectuated. This means your game must be run in a fair and consistent manner – which is why the role of Judge is so important.

3. There are two schools of storytelling in RPGs. In directed storytell-
    ing, the gamemaster, like a movie director, is directing the sequence
    of events that will occur with an eye towards achieving particular
    outcomes or expressing particular themes. In emergent storytelling,
    the storytelling is focused on what just happened; it is the memoirs
    of your player's fictional characters, and the history of their fictional
    deeds. Emergent storytelling gives the players agency and therefore is
    the superior school if you agree with the agency theory of fun. Emer-
    gent storytelling requires replacing the idea of a "story arc" with a
    "story web," a collection of linked points of interest in the game world
    that offer multiple avenues of exploration and interaction.

4. When taking up the role of adversary, you must temporarily put aside
    your godlike GM powers and take up the mantle of an antagonist
    with limited abilities. You should challenge your players to the fullest
    extent of the antagonist's powers, running the encounters fairly and
    honestly, even if it means defeating them, but all the while secretly
    hoping the players will succeed in overcoming the challenges.

5. Adversaries in an RPG are beings in a world, not units in a wargame or
    actors in a movie. When you run adversaries, they should act based on
    the information they have in the world, not the information you have
    as GM; they should fight for their own objectives, not for objectives
    you have as GM. Most of all, when running adversaries, you should
    never lose sight of your primary role (judge). You can always win if
    you want to, and you don't prove anything by "beating" the players.

6. Before you begin building a world, decide what rules set you'll be using and what genre you'll be simulating. The choice of rules needs to be made simultaneously with the choice of genre. Some rules really can support multiple (if not all) settings and genres. Other rules sets support particular genres marvelously, but fail spectacularly outside of them. Some rules sets are so narrowly tailored as to support not only just one genre, but just one setting. It's possible to "hack" a rules set to support different genre conventions and settings, but with so many game systems available, and so many other challenges to gamemastering, it's probably better to find a game system that lines up with the genre and setting you want, at least initially, until you're ready to start tinkering with rules.

7. When it comes to world-building, you can choose from two major schools of design: "top down" and "bottom up." Proponents of top-down design are world-focused and like to establish a framework for their world in advance. Proponents of bottom-up design are player-focused and like to flesh out the immediate vicinity of the player characters in great detail while leaving the framework of their world open. Both have great merit. My personal design method, "top-down zoom-in," is a hybrid of two schools. It starts with a light top-down framework (the "mega-setting"), but creates increasing detail as it gets closer to the areas of the setting that the players are most likely to interact with (the "micro-setting" or "sandbox"). To deploy the top-down zoom-in approach, you create about 10 pages of material, including a high concept for your setting, a world map, a historical timeline of contemporary to forgotten history, and a micro-setting within your world where play is going to happen, with its own regional map and recent history. This material can be provided to your players as a reference guide to your new campaign world.

8. Once you've created a player reference guide, it's time to create a gazetteer of the sandbox. For a fantasy sandbox, a gazetteer will typically cover an area roughly 180 miles x 24 miles in extent, within which you should place 45 static points of interest. One-third of these should be settlements, towns and castles of the humans and demi-humans, while the other two-thirds (30) are dungeons, lairs, or special areas. Of the 30 dungeons/lairs, aim for 3 mega-dungeons each designed for about 6-10 sessions of play; 10 dungeons designed for 1-2 sessions of play; and 17 small lairs designed for a half-session of play, i.e. 1 encounter. Place the points of interest on the map with a gradient of challenge based on proximity to civilization. Then write one paragraph of description for each point. Supplement these static points of interest with dynamic lairs customized for the terrain of your sandbox. You can make these up, or use supplements like *One Page Dungeons* or *Lairs & Encounters.*

9. Once you have a sandbox, the next step in your world building is to transform it into a world in motion. A world in motion is one in which effects occur of which the players are not the purposeful or apparent cause. In many cases, the actions of the players will actually be the cause, through triggering, but this might be without their knowledge or intent. There are four basic techniques you can use to put your world in motion: triggered events, wandering NPCs, hand-crafted content, and random events.

10. When it comes time to actually sit down and run an RPG session, a session that's four hours long (about the length of dinner and a movie or a tailgate and football game) is ideal. Find a venue that has a quiet room with comfortable seating and a large table and be sure to reward any player who brings refreshments for others with bonus XP. Give everyone about 10-15 minutes to settle in and renew social ties, then dive into the game. Try to maintain your scheduled duration as a hard deadline, and be sure to leave about 10-15 minutes for a "post game recap" where everyone discusses what happened and what they want to do next.

11. Most problems in role-playing game campaigns arise from one of three sources. First, one or more of the players might be out of step with the overall social dynamic of the rest of the players. There are several different social dynamics, each of which has its own implicit rules that govern how the players behave towards each other. Your job is to make sure everyone in the group is explicitly aware of and agrees to the same social dynamic. Second, one or more players might be out of step with your GM style. If you're running a sandbox and they want a theme park, for instance, they won't be happy. Again, candidness and transparency are the best way to proceed. Finally, one or more players might have moral or political disagreements that surface in play. It's best to discourage real-world political discussion (and other distracting talk, like sports rivalries) from the game table, but sometimes things in game will lead to heated debate. The answer, again, is to be upfront and honest about what style of game you're running. Sometimes you may have to ask a disgruntled player to exit the campaign, and sometimes you might have to step down as GMs. The most important rule is: Don't let friendships be destroyed because you disagree about what you want out of your RPG hobby.

12. Sustaining a successful long-term RPG campaign is the hallmark of the best GMs. You'll have the best chance for success if you can run weekly or bi-weekly sessions, which will require a commitment from you of about 15 hours per week. You'll need a group of four to six players so that you have enough to carry on even if one or two miss a session each week. Make sure your players understand you are not hosting a series of social events. You are starting an intramural sports team and asking them if they'd like to be on the team.

13. As a gamemaster, you're a judge in a very real sense. Think of the game designer as the legislator, the game rules as the civil law, the players as the parties to the trial, and you as the judge, whose decisions about grey areas in the rules set precedent for future rulings. When you are running a long-term campaign, you should remember that every time you issue a ruling, you have added to the "common law" of the game design. You should write down your rulings, and apply them again to similar situations in the future - or distinguish them from prior rulings to explain why they aren't being applied. The very best game-masters do this so consistently that over time that their long-running campaigns begin to develop an entire body of house rules covering the many special situations that have arisen in their campaign.

14. You will be called on to judge decisions every single session, and when your campaign is young, probably every single encounter. The rules lawyers in your group can be counted on to always advocate for their benefit, but you should not do likewise - it will not do to always side with the players, nor always against them. Instead, you must strive to interpret the rules in a consistent way. To do so, you should employ the following canons of statutory interpretation – rules of thumb to guide judging day after day: Your starting point in interpreting rules is always the plain language employed by the game designer. If a rule specifically defines a term, use the defined definition; but in the absence of a defined definition, interpret the term in accordance with the dictionary definition. If the rule is still ambiguous, look at the rule holistically. Terminology in a rule that is ambiguous in isolation may be clarified if the same terminology is used elsewhere in a context that makes its meaning clear, or because only one of the possible meanings is compatible with the rest of the game. Do not interpret different terms within the same rule to mean the same thing, nor the same term within the same rule to mean different things. If the literal interpretation of the words is absurd, the rule must be interpreted to avoid absurdity. If possible, give meaning to every clause and word of a rule; don't assume anything is redundant. Remember that specific rules override general rules.

15. RPG combat can be really fun, but all too often it's dull and un-interesting. To keep combat exciting, deploy high stakes and vivid imagery – the violence and the viscera of a combat encounter. Every fight should put the party at risk of something and the spectacle must be awesome. If there's one place that the art of storytelling can make more difference than any other, it's in RPG combat.

16. Every time a gamemaster picks up the dice, he is toying with fate - the fate of the players, the fate of the adversaries, the fate of the campaign world. When the dice come up in ways that are unexpected or create situations that are uncomfortable or unwanted, the temptation hangs omnipresent to say the dice said something they did not - to fudge. But you should never fudge a meaningful die roll; the desire to fudge is founded on the faulty premise that you need to make sure people have fun It's a mistake to believe that letting a character fail or die destroys fun. It's fudging the dice that destroys fun, by destroying the ability for the players to make meaningful choices. Keep your fudging limited to circumstances where it makes play faster or improves verisi-militude, and never fudge when it impacts the player's agency.

17. Abduction is the secret art of the greatest gamemasters. Abduction is what transforms random tables and wandering monsters into a living, breathing game world. Abduction is what transforms a hodge-podge of materials into a coherent campaign. It is the art of finding expla-nations that make the campaign better. You must study this art, and master it. To make abduction work for you, take advantage of random content generators, adaptations of other sources of content, or rely on the endlessly conspiratorial imaginations of your players. Once you've mastered the art of abduction, you can use it to run entire adventures on the fly.

18. When you're mastered the art of building and running RPGs, it's time to start creating smash-ups that are uniquely customized to your taste. The key to a successful smash-up lies in identifying a rule mechanic or setting element from one game that somehow fits into the framework of the rules or setting of another game and then importing the rule mechanic or setting element from the first game into the second game. Once you know to start looking for smash-up hooks, your collection of RPGs transforms from games you probably won't ever play to systems for the smashing.

What You Can Do for the RPG Hobby

I began this book by declaring myself a tabletop patriot, one who asks not what RPGs can do for me, but what I can do for RPGs. This book was my answer. Now I ask you to do the same.

The tabletop RPG is the most wonderful hobby in the world. There is no other pastime that so successfully combines creativity, imagination, and strategic thinking with friendship, camaraderie, and teamwork. Look to any creative field today and you will see top talent who were inspired by tabletop RPGs. Firefly would not have existed without Traveller. Game of Thrones would not have appeared with GURPS. And for every Joss Whedon and George R.R. Martin, there are a thousand other gamers equally inspired if less famous. There are few other hobbies that will inspire a reluctant student to even try to master mathematics, read mythology, or study architecture; there are none at all, save ours, that will inspire all three.

In a postmodern society that increasingly leaves everyone alienated and alone in front of their computer screens, tabletop RPGs can bring people together. In a world of nihilistic materialism, tabletop RPGs can remind us that there are things worth fighting for with honor and courage. In dark days and bright days, tabletop RPGs offer a steady source of friend-ship and a ready canvas for the imagination.

I hope that you find the ideas in this book to be helpful in becoming a gamemaster. But more than that, I hope that you find the ideas in this book inspiring. I hope that they inspire you to start a new tabletop RPG campaign – to recruit new players - to pour forth your creativity and share it with them and together re-live the days of high adventure.

AFTERWORD

If you've enjoyed this book, you might also enjoy my game system, *Adventurer Conqueror King System* (*ACKS*) and its supplements. Sign up for my Autarch newsletter by sending an email to alex@autarch.co and I will send you a **free PDF copy** of the *Lairs & Encounters* supplement I mention in Chapter 8. You can find all of my other products at www.autarch.co and at https://www.drivethrurpg.com/browse/pub/4277/Autarch.

P.S. Don't forget to read the Appendix! Turn the page.

APPENDIX A
All About Alignment

In the dark under-city below the caverns of Celadon, desperation gripped the hearts of the heroes. "If we don't find the Black Balm of Beelzebub by dawn, the City of Falcondale will be destroyed!" exclaimed Ariel.

"We'll do what must be done, then," the paladin replied, his voice like steel. He slammed his warhammer down, shattering like walnuts the fingers of his hapless Drow captive. "There's more where that came from," the grim knight said. "Now tell me where the Balm is!"

For a moment, there was nothing but agonized wailing in the air, but it stopped suddenly, and the Drow looked thoughtful. "You know, actually, you can't do this, Bob." The dark elf's Midwestern accent was out of place in the catacombs. "See, you're Lawful Good, and Lawful Good people don't torture. In fact, I think you just lost your Paladin status for doing an evil deed. Let me check the Player's Handbook."

"What? That's ridiculous. What would be evil would be for me to let hundreds of thousands of people die for the sake of a few mashed fingers that a Heal spell will take care of in 6 seconds," the paladin snorted.

"Well, I disagree. Torture is always evil, and it doesn't matter if you heal the wounds. I mean, in Gitmo, those guys they were water-boarding didn't drown, but it was still torture."

"What are you talking about? Water-boarding wasn't torture. It was enhanced interrogation! And even if it was torture, that doesn't make it evil…"

Ah, alignment. Has any rule in *Dungeons & Dragons* caused more arguments? Ever since Gary Gygax first decided to make paladins the most powerful fighters in the game provided they followed a strict alignment code, the problems of alignment have bedeviled players and gamemasters alike.

Alignment isn't an issue every gamemaster must learn to deal with – a lot of games don't even have an alignment system at all – so it didn't make sense to give alignment its own chapter. But I couldn't just ignore alignment. The two most popular RPGs (*D&D 5E* and *Pathfinder*) both use alignment systems, and so do most of their epigones and competitors. Hence, in this appendix – which is totally not a chapter – we're going to tackle the thorny issue of alignment and try to make sense of it all.

ALIGNMENT AS ALLEGIANCE

The simplest system of alignment is "alignment as allegiance," meaning that a character's alignment is simply a statement of which side he is on in some struggle existential to the campaign world. In a World War II RPG, the alignments could be Allied, Axis, and Neutral. In a *Star Wars* RPG, the alignments could be Alliance, Imperial, and Mercenary. In a *Mad Max*-style post-apocalyptic RPG, the alignments could be Settler, Raider, and Drifter. In a US politics RPG, the alignments could be Democrat, Republican, and Swing (or is it Republican, Democrat, and Swing?)

Under this alignment system, a character's personal virtues and vices don't matter, only his allegiance to the cause. In a World War II context, if your character is a nasty piece of work that gets off on fear and likes to carve up the flesh of his defeated foes, it doesn't matter. So long as he fights bravely for the Allies, he's a good guy. (*Inglourious Basterds*, I'm looking at you!) Likewise, if your character is an upstanding, honorable, disciplined soldier like Erwin Rommel who writes books, loves his wife, and gives to charity, it doesn't matter. If he fights for the Axis he's a bad guy. If that's too historical, then consider that you needn't mourn the death of the contractors on the Death Star because they were aligned Imperial.

"Alignment as allegiance" was the very first alignment system in the very first RPG. Consider that the word "alignment" is not a term that has anything to do with ethics or morals when used in contexts outside of role-playing games. Rather, alignment is mostly used in two ways, neither tied to morality: 1) to refer to something that we need for our car ("I need to get my car's alignment adjusted"); 2) to refer to which side in a conflict a nation chooses ("The alignment of Italy with Germany created the Axis of Steel that was to terrorize Europe").

In the latter reference we find the origin of the term: Alignment in *D&D* originally referred to which side in a conflict a character chose! *Chainmail*, the miniature wargame from which *D&D* descended, provided an order of battle dividing all creatures into "Law," "Neutral," and "Chaos." These were factions within the wargame, just as in a wargame about World War II there would be "Allied," "Neutral," and "Axis" factions. When *Chainmail* individualized to *D&D*, the individual character's choice of a faction became known as his "Alignment," as in indicating which of the warring factions the character had "aligned" himself with. The only suggestion of a moral context is seen in the fact that presumably pleasant creatures like treants and unicorns were said to be aligned with Law, while the likes of evil high priests, vampires, and orcs were said to be aligned with Chaos.

Why did *Chainmail* and *D&D* use Law and Chaos instead of Good and Evil to describe the warring factions? Many people mistakenly credit this to Michael Moorcock and the Elric series, but the origin actually comes from Poul Anderson's classic *Three Hearts and Three Lions*:

> [He] got the idea that a perpetual struggle went on between primeval forces of Law and Chaos... Humans were the chief agents on earth of Law, though some of them were so only unconsciously, and some, witches and warlocks, and evildoers, had sold out to Chaos. A few nonhuman beings also stood for Law. Ranged against them were almost the whole Middle World, which seemed to include realms like Faerie, Trollheim, and the Giants - an actual creation of Chaos. Wars among men, such as the long-drawn struggle between the Saracens and the Holy Empire, aided Chaos; under Law, all men would live in peace and order and that liberty which only Law could give meaning. But this was so alien to Middle Worlders that they were forever working to prevent it and extend their own shadowy dominion."

A similar primeval struggle seems to show up in almost every game or genre, representing the war between civilization and barbarism, Western "white hats" v. "black hats," and so on. It is the implicit alignment system of pretty much every superhero game. As a system, it's exceptionally simple to define, as all it really requires is being able to identify two competing sides that a character is fighting for (if not willing to die for any side, the character is neutral). It maintains the sense of grand struggle that is provided by an over-arching alignment system, a sense that the character's decisions are part of something larger than himself. And it achieves all these goals while maintaining maximum flexibility for the player characters to develop their personalities without concern that they'll violate their alignment.

Because of its many virtues, the "alignment as allegiance approach is what I adopted for my own *Adventurer Conqueror King System* rules.

> In the *Adventurer Conqueror King System*, your character will enter a world of ceaseless violent struggle, where civilization is ever-assailed by forces intent on its destruction. In this perilous realm, he will be called to choose a side: Will he pledge to defend civilization and its allies against those who seek to destroy it? Will he sell his sword to any who can offer fame or fortune? Or will he become an agent of entropy and destruction undermining peace and order? This choice is called Alignment, and the three choices are Lawful, Neutral, and Chaotic.
>
> **Law:** Lawful beings believe that civilization is worth fighting for. Despite its vices and villainies, civilization must be defended against those who would destroy it. Lawful beings tend to see wars among civilizations as aiding the cause of Chaos, and so they seek peace among Lawful civilizations where possible. However, Lawful characters are not pacifists, nor are they necessarily altruists. Indeed, most would think something was wrong with a hero who turned down fame and fortune; chests of gold, magnificent weapons, comely consorts, and grants of land are, after all, the rightful rewards for great deeds of valor on behalf of Law.
>
> **Neutrality:** Neutral beings generally enjoy the benefits of law and civilization, but it is not something they directly fight for. They tend to focus on their own ends, whether those are family, fame, fortune, pleasure, or power. A Neutral mercenary might be found fighting on behalf of Law or

Chaos; a neutral farmer tends his crops and pays his taxes, whether to the Patriarch or the Lich-King.

Chaos: Chaotic beings actively seek to destroy civil society. Chaotic characters are often madmen or cultists of forgotten, chthonic gods. To the extent they have any order at all, societies of Chaotic characters are ruled by force and fear, and are often characterized by all manner of corruption and vice. Even decadent Lawful civilizations at least pay homage to civilizing virtue, but chaotic civilizations embrace their corruption.

Note that a character's choice of Alignment doesn't determine whether or not he takes care of his children, cheats on his wife, or steals from the merchant's guild. It is concerned only with the weighty issue of where his allegiance lies in the grand struggles of existence. To have an alignment of Lawful or Chaotic is to have chosen a side in this perpetual struggle. Many people, choosing no side, are Neutral, although it is important to remember that most Neutrals still want the protection of Law even though they are not willing to die for it. (To paraphrase George Orwell, Neutral humans sleep peaceably in their beds at night only because Lawful heroes stand ready to do violence on their behalf.)

There are two downsides to "alignment as allegiance" system. The first is that there has to be some sort of existential conflict within the campaign, within which characters give steady allegiance to one side or another. It would be hard to use alignment as allegiance in *Cyberpunk 2020*, for instance (everyone's alignment would just be "Self!"). The second is that the system does not provide any role-playing guidance for how the character might behave. For instance, despite their vast differences in behavior and code, "alignment as allegiance" puts Superman, Batman, and the Punisher all on the same side (Hero). Because of these limitations, "alignment as allegiance" was soon replaced in the *D&D* line by a new system – "alignment as philosophy."

THERE REALLY IS AN AXIS OF EVIL

The "alignment as philosophy" or "dual axis" system divides moral behavior into two axes: The Lawful/Neutral/Chaotic axis and the Good/Neutral/Evil axis. A character's alignment is composed of one element from each axis, creating combinations such as "Lawful Good" and "Neutral Evil." According to the d20 rules, these encompass "a broad range of personal philosophies" that are "a tool for developing your character's identity." The dual axis system is so popular that it has evolved past its origins in *Advanced Dungeons & Dragons* into a meme factory of posters, t-shirts, and homages in everything from *Warhammer* to *Fable II's* dual morality and purity axes.

That sounds well and good; yet most gamers, having not studied moral philosophy, simply lack the vocabulary to assess what good or evil means, let alone law or chaos. Even the simplest assessments often lead to long arguments: If a Lawful Good hero tells a lie in order to save someone's life, has he violated his alignment? If Luke Skywalker really did restore order to the galaxy along with Darth, would that have been Evil? Is *Highlander's* Kurgan being Chaotic when he madly drives down the wrong side of the road in New York City, or is he just being an idiot? Confusion is nowadays so great that *TV Tropes* has pages documenting and ridiculing the problems of Lawful Anal and Chaotic Stupid characters. To avoid the Stupid, some modern gamers now eschew alignment altogether, consigning it to the trash bin of game design.

Despite the problems of alignment, throwing it out is the wrong move for most campaigns. The classic struggle of good versus evil appears repeatedly in myth, legend, and fiction. To ignore alignment is to ignore the most powerful themes that underlie gaming's popular genres. *The Lord of the Rings* is hardly a gripping story if the Reign of Sauron and Aragorn are morally equivalent. Even the most deconstructionist of epic fantasy works - George R. R. Martin's *Game of Thrones* - still offers us examples of true *D&D*-style Chaotic Evil.

With morality hardcoded into the genres they emulate, the "alignment as philosophy" is worthy of use in play. So can sense be made of it? The answer is yes! The past 3,000 years of moral theory may not have led us to world peace, but Aristotle, Bentham, Kant, and Nietzsche have at least provided us some answers to our D&D dilemmas.

Let's start with the basics: A moral code is a system of values that differentiates between good and bad and/or right and wrong. Over the past three thousand years, moral philosophers have developed a staggering amount of moral codes based on differing assessments of the objectivity, perspective, scope, and substance of moral codes. Of the vast range of possible moral questions one can ask, however, solving our alignment dilemma really only asks us to answer two questions: How do you judge the "goodness" of an action? And who are the proper beneficiaries of "good" behavior, i.e. whose "good" are we talking about? The answer to the first question will establish a person's place on the spectrum of Law and Chaos; the answer to the second question, their place on the spectrum of Good and Evil.

It's All Clear Once You Realize Lawful Just Means Deontological

So our first question is "how you judge the 'goodness' of an action?" Moral philosophy offers us three main answers: By the action itself (deontological); by the consequences of the action (consequentialist); and by the character of the action (aretological). These three map nicely to Lawful, Chaotic, and Neutral, as will be shown below.

Deontological, or rules-based, ethics judge the goodness of an action based on whether the action itself adhered to a set of principles developed in advance. Most religions include deontological ethical systems: When the Ten Commandments say "you shall not steal," it means that you shall not steal, *period*. It doesn't matter if your family is starving and you need the bread; stealing is wrong because the Commandment says so. Some secular systems are also deontological. During the Enlightenment, Immanuel Kant developed his incredibly influential deontological system based on Categorical Imperatives, or maxims for rightful action. Murray Rothbard's non-aggression principle is a famous libertarian deontological system. As a result of their philosophy, deontologists generally believe that rules should be obeyed; promises should be kept; processes should be followed; and that ends *never* justify means. They are, in short, Lawful!

In contrast to the strict principles of deontological ethics, Chaotic characters believe in consequentialist or act-based ethics: They judge the goodness of an action based on the consequences of the action. To a consequentialist, rightness or wrongness is judged by the result of the deed, not the deed itself. Jeremy Bentham's act-based utilitarianism, which instructs its adherents to act to produce the greatest good for the greatest number, is the most famous consequentialist moral system. Consequentialists are results-oriented. They believe that promises can be broken, rules ignored, and laws overridden, because the end always justify the means. They are the essence of Chaotic, prone to answering claims that they've broken a contract by saying "I am altering the deal - pray I don't alter it any further."

In between these two positions is a third way, which could be called aretological, or character-based ethics. To an aretologist, the goodness of an action is judged based on the character trait which motivated the action.

While they ultimately judge the rightness or wrongness of deeds in their totality by their consequences, they believe that it is impossible to predict what the consequences are likely to be in most circumstances. Instead, we should generally behaving in accordance with particular character traits (the "virtues"), habits, or rules of thumb which tend to promote these desirable consequences overall. John Stuart Mill's rules-based utilitarianism and Aristotle's virtue ethics both lead to similar reasoning. In an aretological system, the moral character traits, habits, or rules of thumb should be followed unless there is a strong reason for not doing so. Such people will generally follow the rules and keep their promises, but not so strictly as Lawful characters; they may act on a case-by-case basis when circumstances dictate, though not with such disdain for custom and law as Chaotics. They are, in short, Neutrals. When you ponder whether it's permissible to run a red light when there's obviously nobody around, you're thinking like a Neutral. (The Lawful person would never consider it, and the Chaotic person drove through as soon as he knew it was safe.)

These may seem like subtle or esoteric distinctions, but in practice they can lead to radically different behavior. Consider, for example, a busy investment banker who promises his son that he will not miss his 13th birthday. A major client, however, wants the banker to travel on that day; if he refuses, he will lose a lot of money on the deal – an amount equal to his son's college fund! Let's assume that the banker wants to do the right thing for his son. If Lawful, the banker will certainly honor his promise. If Chaotic, the banker might honor his promise, but he might also conclude that the consequences of losing that much money are too damaging to his son's future, and take the meeting. In this example, it's not coincidental that the Lawful banker *will* do something, while the Chaotic *might* do something. Lawful characters have reliable behavior patterns that are governed by stable rules. Chaotic characters do not.

Is it a Circle of Life, or a Circle of Strife?

Having identified how we judge the "goodness" of actions, and thereby identifying Lawful, Neutral, and Chaotic philosophies, the second question we must answer is who the proper beneficiaries of "good" behavior are. In short, whose "good" are we talking about? The answer to this question will correlate with an element on the Good and Evil axis.

To frame this discussion, let's turn to Peter Singer's theory of the "expanding circle of morality," in which each individual has a different circle that he takes account of when evaluating what's good. At its narrowest point, this simply means a man asking "what's good for me?" A broader circle might include "what's good for me, my family, my neighborhood, or my tribe?" A vastly broader circle might include "what's good for all mankind" or even "what's good for all life on earth?" Within the circle, the individual may treat everyone equally, or may elevate certain interests above those of another. An individual who treats everyone equally within his circle has a flat circle, while one who discounts the interests of others the further away they are on the circle has a sloped circle.

This concept of the expanding moral circle elegantly maps onto the *Dungeons & Dragons* alignments. Good characters have very broad, flat moral circles that generally encompass all other Good creatures. Such a character feels an obligation to help, serve, and benefit others, even at the sacrifice of their self-interest.

Neutral characters have modest, sloped moral circles that encompass themselves, their loved ones, and their tribe, city, country, or race, at an increasing slope of disinterest as the circle expands. The ancient Arab maxim "me against my brother; my brother and I against our cousin; my brother, my cousin and I against the stranger" expresses a Neutral sentiment. Objectivism, which demands that "I will never live for the sake of another man, nor ask another man to live for mine," is another expression of Neutrality. (A Good person would live for others; an Evil person would have no compunction against asking another man to give his life for him.)

Finally, Evil characters have narrow moral circles that encompass themselves and perhaps their closest friends or family, and then sharply slope into total disinterest; many Evil characters may indeed have a circle of one, with others valued only as useful tools or object of affection rather than as moral ends. For *D&D's* Evil, we can look to Friedrich Nietzsche, who claims that to achieve greatness, a man must "lack congeniality and good-naturedness" and "consider everyone he meets on his way either as a means or as a delay and obstacle;" such a man, with a "strong and domineering nature" "want[s] no sympathetic hearts, but servants and tools."

An interesting edge case occurs with characters whose moral circle changes with their emotional state. A king given over to a vengeful rage might make an Evil decision based on a narrow moral circle defined by his fury ("I'll destroy your entire realm!") while that same king, when calm and happy, might well make a Good decision based on the welfare of his people. Characters whose moral circle fluctuates usually are described based on their average moral circle with a tendency under the influence of strong emotion (e.g. "Neutral with Evil tendencies").

GOOD IS GOOD, EXCEPT WHEN ITS BAD

The Nietzsche quote above comes from his book, *Beyond Good and Evil*, which raises the interesting point: In the real world, people who would be Evil in *D&D* tend not to think of themselves as "evil." Our friend Nietzsche explained this by arguing that there were two basic ways of labeling moral behaviors. The first system of morality, associated with the Heroic Age of

Greece, contrasted "good" (strong, healthy, wealthy, powerful) with "bad" (weak, sick, poor, pathetic). The heroes of the *Iliad* or *Odyssey*, who can seem downright sociopathic to modern readers, were paragons of heroic virtue under their ancient moral code. The second system of morality, associated by Nietzsche with the Judeo-Christian tradition, contrasts "good" (restrained, kind, charitable, humble) with "evil" (aggressive, cruel, greedy, proud). Nietzsche's belief was that Judeo-Christian "evil" morality leads to what the ancients called "good" behavior (powerful and rich), while Judeo-Christian "good" morality leads to what the ancients called "bad" behavior (meek and slavish).

Because it's a game originally developed by writers from the Judeo-Christian tradition, it's not altogether surprising that *Dungeons & Dragons* has assigned its metaphysical Good and Evil to approximately correlate with Judeo-Christian "good" and "evil" - indeed, the game's alignments can probably best be understood as being written from a Lawful Good perspective.

However, in your own campaign, you should probably consider how societies that aren't Lawful Good label the alignments. Here are some suggestions:

- Chaotic Evil societies might translate the Good/Evil axis as the Foolish/Sensible axis, and the Law/Chaos axis as the Dogmatic/Pragmatic axis. A Chaotic Evil dread lord would see himself as Pragmatic and Sensible, while his Lawful Good foe is Dogmatic and Foolish. ("The fool throws his life away for others who would never do the same for him!")

- ◦ Lawful Evil societies might translate the Good/Evil axis as the Slavish/Masterful axis, and the Law/Chaos axis as the Honorable/Dishonorable axis. An Honorably Masterful noble would have little time for a Dishonorably Slavish rabble rouser and his priggish peasant uprising.

- ◦ True Neutral societies might translate the Good/Evil axis as the Vainglorious/Virtuous/Vicious axis, and the Law/Chaos axis as the Rigid Morals/Proper Morals/Loose Morals axis. They'd consider themselves Virtuous and Proper, Lawful Good paladins to be Rigid and Vainglorious, and Chaotic Evil blackguards to be Loose and Vicious.

ALIGNMENT AS ATTITUDE

Having fielded this system in play, I'm fairly confident it's a workable approach to understanding alignment both in theory and practice. It successfully explains the differing D&D alignments as different moral frameworks from Lawful Good's deontological altruism to Neutral's aretological egoism to Chaotic Evil's consequentialist nihilism. But this result, which might be called "alignment as philosophy," is highly abstract.

Fortunately, there's another system you can turn to if what you want is a simple methodology that can differentiate between, e.g., Superman and the Punisher without requiring an understanding of Kant. If the dual-axis system was "alignment as philosophy," explaining the differing D&D alignments as different moral frameworks, this system could be called "alignment as attitude," and it appears in all the Palladium Books Megaverse RPGs. By virtue of the great popularity of Palladium's Rifts and its ilk (Robotech, Heroes Unlimited, etc.) these rules are probably the second-most popular alignment system in tabletop gaming, and even more probably the closest in practice to how players actually think about and use alignment in play.

Rifts and its relatives describe alignment as the characters' "attitudes and moral principles." These alignments are organized along a single axis, good/selfish/evil, with two to three alignments of each type. Each alignment is assigned a highly descriptive name: The good alignments are "principled" and "scrupulous," the selfish alignments are "unprincipled" and "anarchistic," and the evil alignments are "aberrant," "miscreant," and "diabolic." Each of these alignments is further defined by a short set of guidelines that describe the habitual behavior of its adherents. For instance, both principled and aberrant characters "always keep their word," while anarchist characters "may keep their word" and diabolic characters "rarely keep their word and have no honor." Miscreant characters "will betray a friend if it serves their needs," while diabolic characters "will betray a friend because you can always find another friend." Anarchistic characters "do not work within groups and tend to do as they please despite orders to the contrary," while unprincipled characters "work with groups, especially if its serves their needs, is profitable, and/or they're in the limelight."

Because the names are descriptive and concrete, and the guidelines are so clear, players can instantly grasp what it means to be "principled" or "anarchistic." It's much easier to grasp a concrete set of guidelines than to try to grapple with what it means to be "lawful good" or, god forbid, "chaotic neutral." It's also much easier to assign famous characters into this alignment system (i.e., without much debate one can see that Superman is "principled," Batman is "scrupulous," and The Punisher is "aberrant"), which is helpful both in gaming in popular settings and also in generally setting expectations. So if the "alignment as allegiance" system is too simple, and the "alignment as philosophy" system is too abstract, the "alignment as attitude" system is a fast, simple, and effective alternative.

The downside to the Palladium approach is inherent in its strength; the alignments really are just habitual behaviors. It removes the metaphysical meaning of the alignments entirely. It is hard to envision heroes rallying to the cause of Principledness in the way that we imagine the heroes of Law rallying to the angels of order. Nor is there a sense of metaphysical karma: Nothing in the Palladium system marks out a Principled character as anything other than a schmuck who lets the bad guys take advantage of his honor and gentleness.

In practice, you can overcome this if you're willing to "hack the system" and correlate the Palladium alignments with the D&D alignments:

- Principled - Lawful Good

- Scrupulous - Chaotic Good

- Unprincipled - Neutral (with good tendencies)

- Anarchistic - Chaotic Neutral

- Aberrant - Lawful Evil

- Miscreant - Neutral Evil

- Diabolic - Chaotic Evil

You might tinker with the specific behaviors for each, and add new ones to fill in the gaps ("Bureaucratic" for Lawful Neutral, for instance), but that's half the fun.

Made in the USA
Columbia, SC
07 December 2019

84511648R00085